WASHINGTON WILDLIFE VIEWING GUIDE

Joe La Tourrette

FALCON®

ACKNOWLEDGMENTS

The following individuals provided important guidance during the production of this guide. Their interest and expertise was invaluable in helping the author screen site nominations, select most-sought-after species, and develop and refine site descriptions: Thais Bock, Federal Way, Washington; Don Clift, Washington Department of Natural Resources; Steve Dunn, U.S. Bureau of Reclamation; Helen Engle, Tacoma, Washington; Betsy Gabel, Washington State Tourism Division; Rich Haire, U.S. Fish and Wildlife Service; Neal Hedges, U.S. Bureau of Land Management; Ann Herdrick, Odessa Economic Development Council; Steve Jenks, Washington Department of Fisheries; Lou Jurs, U.S. Bureau of Land Management; Bill Melton, Washington Department of Transportation; Janet O' Mara, Washington Parks and Recreation Commission; Betty Rodrick, Washington Department of Wildlife; Jeff Skriletz, Washington Department of Wildlife; and Susan Waidman, U.S. Army Corps of Engineers.

In addition to those mentioned above, the following people contributed significantly to the completion of this project: Patty Carter, for lining up initial corporate funding for the project; Wally Miller of Miller and Associates, Olympia, for providing encouragement, office space, and logistical support; Pat "Sunny" Walter, for visiting, photographing, and writing up many of the sites on her own time; and Kathy, Julie, and Katrina La Tourrette, for spending many cold and wet weekends visiting wildlife viewing sites.

Special thanks to Mark G. Lewis of Sea Quest Expeditions/Zoetic Research for providing the cover photo. Sea Quest Expeditions/Zoetic Research, P.O. Box 2424, Friday Harbor, WA 98250, (206) 378-5767

The following references were very helpful in the production of this viewing guide:

Osborne, Richard et al. 1988. *A Guide to Marine Mammals of Greater Puget Sound*. Anacortes, Washington: Island Publishers.

Scott, James W. and Melly A. Reuling. 1986. *Washington Public Shore Guide—Marine Waters*. Washington Department of Ecology: University of Washington Press.

Steelquist, Robert U. 1989. *Ferryboat Field Guide*. Helena, Montana: American Geographic Publishing.

Wahl, Terence R. and Dennis R. Paulson. 1991 (revised edition). *A Guide to Bird Finding in Washington*. Bellingham, Washington: T.R. Wahl.

Author and State Project Manager
Joe La Tourrette

National Watchable Wildlife Program Coordinator
Kate Davies, Defenders of Wildlife

Illustrations
Suze Woolf

Front cover photo: Roosevelt Elk, CHUCK AND GRACE BARTLETT,
Back cover photo: Little Spokane River Natural Area, PAT O'HARA

CONTENTS

Printed in Korea.
Library of Congress Number 92-053272
ISBN 1-56044-150-X

FALCON®

PROJECT SPONSORS

DEFENDERS OF WILDLIFE is a national, nonprofit organization of more than 200,000 members and supporters dedicated to preserving the natural abundance and diversity of wildlife and its habitat. A one-year membership is $20 and includes six issues of the bimonthly magazine. Write or call Defenders of Wildlife, 1244 Nineteenth St., NW, Washington, DC 20036, (202) 659-9510 or visit our website at www.defenders.org.

U.S. FOREST SERVICE manages 9,149,452 acres in Washington for many uses. National forest land ranges from coastal rainforest to the dry ponderosa pine forests on the eastern slope of the Cascades. National forest lands are open year-round for public recreation, including camping, hiking, hunting, fishing, and of course wildlife viewing. Different national forests and ranger districts have different rules governing fires, overnight camping, and seasonal road closures. Check with local Forest Service offices for more specific information on public use and local wildlife viewing opportunities.

ACKERLEY COMMUNICATIONS is a national multimedia advertising company headquartered in Seattle, Washington, with interests in outdoor advertising, broadcasting, airport display advertising, and professional sports entertainment. Because the natural beauty of the Northwest is a gift many of our companies enjoy, we are pleased to sponsor the Washington Watchable Wildlife program to help increase public support in preserving our quality of life. The Watchable Wildlife program is a community project that supports our corporate giving goals: effective, measurable results that improve life in the cities and towns where we live and work.

WASHINGTON DEPARTMENT OF WILDLIFE owns, leases, or manages over 850,000 acres of land for wildlife habitat and wildlife related public recreation in Washington. Habitat managed by WDW ranges from prime wetlands around Puget Sound to large tracts of wintering habitat for deer and elk on the east slope of the Cascades. WDW manages half of their land cooperatively with the USFS, USFWS, USBR, and the Washington Department of Natural Resources. WDW lands are generally open year-round for wildlife viewing, hiking, and other outdoor recreation, as well as hunting and sport fishing during established seasons. WDW lands provide some of the best viewing in the state for deer, elk, and waterfowl. A hunting, fishing, or conservation license is required to use some WDW lands and water access areas; these lands are posted.

THOUSAND TRAILS and NATIONAL AMERICAN CORPORATION (NACO) own and operate a total of sixty membership camping resorts. Thousand Trails' thirty-six membership camping resorts in fifteen states and British Columbia now make up the nation's largest network of private membership campgrounds serving approximately 90,000 member families. NACO operates twenty-four membership campgrounds in twelve states serving more than

82,000 member families, and eight condominium resort communities in seven states serving more than 40,000 resort property owners. Both Thousand Trails and NACO are supporting the Watchable Wildlife program and are dedicated to increasing the awareness of conservation and the environment. For more information, contact Thousand Trails and NACO, 12301 NE 10th Place, Bellevue, WA 98005, (206) 455-3155.

THE NATIONAL FISH AND WILDLIFE FOUNDATION, chartered by Congress to stimulate private giving to conservation, is an independent not-for-profit organization. Using federally funded challenge grants, it forges partnerships between the public and private sectors to conserve the nation's fish, wildlife, and plants. National Fish and Wildlife Foundation, 18th and C Street NW, Washington, DC 20240, (202) 208-4051.

WASHINGTON DEPARTMENT OF FISHERIES is responsible for the conservation and management of all salmon, marine fish, and shellfish in Washington. WDF manages these resources for both commercial harvest and recreational enjoyment. WDF does not manage a large land base, although many WDF hatcheries, rearing facilities, and natural spawning areas are open to the public. WDF has identified a number of sites in this wildlife viewing guide where the public can see Pacific salmon migrating or spawning in tributary streams of the Columbia River and Puget Sound.

U.S. FISH AND WILDLIFE SERVICE administers twenty-one national wildlife refuges in Washington. National wildlife refuges are generally open for public enjoyment, although most have permanent or seasonal restrictions on access, hunting, and other recreational activities that might adversely affect wildlife. Admission at some refuges is free; others charge a small day-use fee. National wildlife refuges in Washington offer some of the best wildlife viewing opportunities in the state, especially for migratory waterfowl in the fall, winter, and spring.

U.S. BUREAU OF LAND MANAGEMENT administers about 340,000 acres of land in Washington. The BLM is responsible for managing public lands, and their resources, under a multiple-use mandate. Most BLM lands are open for public recreation, with appropriate restrictions to protect soil, vegetation, and wildlife. The BLM has recently initiated a Watchable Wildlife program and many of these sites are included in this guide.

Other important contributors include:

U.S. Bureau of Reclamation • U.S. Army Corps of Engineers
Plum Creek Timber Company • Washington Water Power
Washington State Parks and Recreation Commission
Washington Department of Transportation • Eddie Bauer, Inc.

INTRODUCTION

Whether you are an occasional visitor or a permanent resident, you will discover that Washington is a wonderful place to observe wildlife. From the temperate rainforest of Olympic National Park and the islands of Puget Sound to the Channeled Scablands of eastern Washington, there is an incredible variety of year-round and seasonal opportunities to see and learn about the wildlife and ecology of the Pacific Northwest. With Washington's varied topography and its location on the north Pacific Coast, the diversity of habitats and wildlife is very high. Because Washington is the smallest of all the Western states—less than half the size of Montana—a broad range of wildlife experiences can be packed into relatively short distances and time periods.

This viewing guide was designed for both the casual viewer and the serious wildlife watcher. The ninety sites featured in this guide were carefully selected to reflect the rich diversity of the state, as well as a range of desirable wildlife experiences. Some sites are located in urban areas; others require driving to the mountains, the ocean, or the high desert of eastern Washington. Some sites have good public facilities; others are primitive. All ninety sites are open to the public and all offer at least a reasonable chance of viewing wildlife in its natural habitat.

The job of selecting ninety sites was not easy. More than 300 good viewing areas were initially recommended by federal and state agencies and local chambers of commerce. Site visits by the author and careful screening by an interagency steering committee made it possible to narrow these recommendations to the sites included in this viewing guide.

Many of Washington's most beautiful and interesting wildlife species are migratory, and some of the best viewing opportunities come at times of the year considered off-season for other outdoor pursuits. But this guide, along with a sense of adventure and a willingness to be at the right place at the right time, will help you see and experience some of America's most beautiful and interesting wildlife.

THE NATIONAL WATCHABLE WILDLIFE PROGRAM

In 1986, the President's Commission on American Outdoors identified wildlife recreation as one of the nation's most popular outdoor activities. Public interest in wildlife continues to grow rapidly at both the national and state levels. A 1988 Washington survey showed that eighty-four percent of state residents regularly participate in some form of wildlife-related recreation.

At the same time that general interest in wildlife is growing, recreational demand is shifting away from hunting and other traditional pursuits into programs and activities that are oriented to observing wildlife in its natural habitat. A national survey commissioned by the U.S. Fish and Wildlife Service in 1985 found that 135 million Americans participated in some form of wildlife viewing, feeding, or photography as a primary or secondary recreational activity.

As public demand grows, and as wildlife habitat is altered or lost to development, the cost of providing such recreational opportunities is escalating. For many years, hunters and anglers supplied most of the funding for wildlife conservation through license fees and excise taxes on firearms and fishing tackle. This revenue base is no longer growing and the fees are inadequate to meet current or future demands. Thus efforts are under way in every state and at the national level to develop new funding mechanisms for wildlife conservation and recreation.

The National Watchable Wildlife Program was officially initiated in 1990 with the signing of a Memorandum of Understanding between eight federal land management agencies, the International Association of Fish and Wildlife Agencies, and four national conservation groups, including Defenders of Wildlife. The Washington project was started in 1991 with a decision to develop a state-wide system of Watchable Wildlife sites and to develop and publish this Washington Wildlife Viewing Guide. The program is designed to help meet public demand for wildlife recreation, to increase public awareness of the habitat needs of wildlife, and to build a new base of public support for wildlife conservation.

With publication of this guide, site enhancement will begin across the state. This process will include development of facilities, such as parking and nature trails, and interpretive displays. Not every site appearing in this guide will be fully developed by the time of publication, but the process is under way.

As the National Watchable Wildlife Program expands in the future, new wildlife viewing sites not found in this guide will appear in Washington. All sites will be marked with the familiar brown and white road sign featuring a binoculars logo. Please check carefully the directions to each site featured in this book, as highway signs may refer to more than one viewing site.

When visiting exceptionally large viewing sites, such as a national park, please be advised that highway signs may appear only at the park entrance. If this is the case, please stop at a park visitors center for assistance in locating specific viewing opportunities mentioned in this guide.

BIODIVERSITY IN WASHINGTON

Biodiversity is a concept that has long been accepted in scientific circles but only recently has come into use by public officials and the media—most recently surrounding the 1992 Earth Summit in Rio de Janeiro, Brazil. Simply put, biodiversity or biological diversity refers to the variety of plant and animal life and the biological processes found in a particular ecosystem or location.

Biodiversity is a function of land form, climate, and all those natural influences that determine soils, vegetation, and wildlife found in an area. Washington's biodiversity is high due to many factors, including its mountainous topography, its exposure to Pacific Ocean currents and weather patterns, and its location on the migratory path of many wildlife species. Washington has seacoast, high steppe desert, all or part of four discrete mountain ranges, and a huge inland sea called Puget Sound. Washington, in fact, contains most of the major ecosystems found in the western United States—all within the borders of a state that is less than half the size of Montana. Some ecosystems, such as the Olympic rainforest and the Channeled Scablands of eastern Washington, are found nowhere else in the United States.

Biodiversity is not a constant. In fact, Washington's biodiversity is affected and compromised every day by human disturbance to natural ecosystems. Much of the state is forested, but only a very small part, about ten percent, has been left unlogged. Estuarine (coastal) wetlands are extremely productive ecosystems, yet more than ninety percent of these wetlands in Puget Sound have been lost since the turn of the century. The irrigated lands of the Columbia Basin traditionally supported nesting and wintering waterfowl, yet up to eighty-five percent of these native grasslands and shrub-steppe desert plant communities have been lost to grazing and agricultural development. As Washington continues to grow and develop, wildlife habitat will be altered and, sometimes, lost forever. When habitat or wildlife is lost, Washington's biodiversity is further altered.

Efforts are under way by government agencies and conservation groups such as Defenders of Wildlife to document Washington's habitats and wildlife so that steps may be taken in the future to maintain our biodiversity for future generations—and to hopefully avoid the painful listing of species such as the Northern spotted owl under the Endangered Species Act.

VIEWING HINTS

Choose your season. Much of Washington's wildlife is migratory and may be seen only at certain times of the year. California gray whales, for instance, are only seen off the Pacific Coast for a few weeks in the spring. Use the wildife index on page 96 to help plan your field trips.

Learn the feeding habits of your quarry. Many species of wildlife can best be seen during the first and last hours of daylight. Many shorebirds, marine birds, and waterfowl follow the tides in their daily feeding cycle.

Use binoculars. A good pair of binoculars or a spotting scope will open up a whole new world of wildlife viewing. With a twenty power spotting scope, for instance, it is possible to see a mountain goat standing 1.5 miles away.

Come prepared. The weather is unpredictable in Washington, especially west of the Cascades, where you should plan for rain in any season. Always consult tide charts in marine waters and intertidal areas. If you travel off the beaten path, make sure you have a good map and enough clothing, water, and food to survive the night if your car breaks down

Move slowly and quietly. There is probably nothing you can do to better improve your chances of seeing wildlife than to slow down or stop periodically. Animals often disappear as you arrive but may return shortly if you are quiet enough. Use your ears to locate birds. Use your peripheral vision to spot movement in trees, thick brush, and water.

Use field guides. Field guides can tell you the best dates to see migratory wildlife. They can also tell you what habitats an animal prefers, when it is active, and what it eats. A few guides are recommended in the Acknowledgments; others are available for every kind of plant and animal found in Washington.

Enjoy wildlife at a distance. Refrain from touching, feeding, or moving too close to animals. Some birds will abandon their nests if they feel threatened. Even something as shy as an opossum may be dangerous if cornered. Young animals that appear to be orphaned usually have parents waiting in the shadows. If you believe an animal is injured, sick, or abandoned, contact the nearest office of the Washington Department of Wildlife.

Wildlife viewing requires patience. Allow yourself enough time in the field. If you arrive at a site expecting to see all the species listed in the site description in one visit, you will likely be disappointed.

Respect the rights of private landowners. Get permission from private landowners before entering their property. Whether you are on private or public land, leave habitat in better condition than you found it. Pick up litter.

HOW TO USE THIS GUIDE

This guide is divided into six geographic regions, each coded a different color for quick reference. Wildlife viewing sites are listed and located on a map at the beginning of each region. Each site includes the following elements to help describe and interpret what may be seen.

Wildlife Symbols: These symbols show the kinds of wildlife most likely seen at each site. They do not include all the species that might occur at a site.

Description: This gives a brief account of the habitat and wildlife found at a site.

Viewing Information: This section expands on the site description and gives the seasonal likelihood of seeing wildlife at the site. It also may include information about access, parking, and WARNINGS in capital letters.

Directions: A full-color map is provided for each site. Roads, nearby towns, access points, and other viewing information can be found on these maps. NOTE: PLEASE SUPPLEMENT THE MAPS IN THIS GUIDE WITH AN UP-TO-DATE WASHINGTON ROAD MAP.

Ownership: Provides the name or abbreviation of the agency, organization, or company that owns or manages the site. The telephone number listed may be used to obtain more information.

Recreation and Facility Symbols: These indicate some of the facilities and opportunities available at each site. The managing agency can provide more information.

SITE OWNER-MANAGER ABBREVIATIONS

ACE	U.S. Army Corps of Engineers
BLM	U.S. Bureau of Land Management
NPS	National Park Service
USBR	U.S. Bureau of Reclamation
USFS	U.S. Forest Service
USFWS	U.S. Fish & Wildlife Service
WDW	Washington Department of Wildlife
WDF	Washington Department of Fisheries
WSP	Washington State Parks and Recreation Commission
WDNR	Washington Department of Natural Resources
WDOT	Washington Department of Transportation
WDOE	Washington Department of Ecology

WASHINGTON

Wildlife Viewing Areas

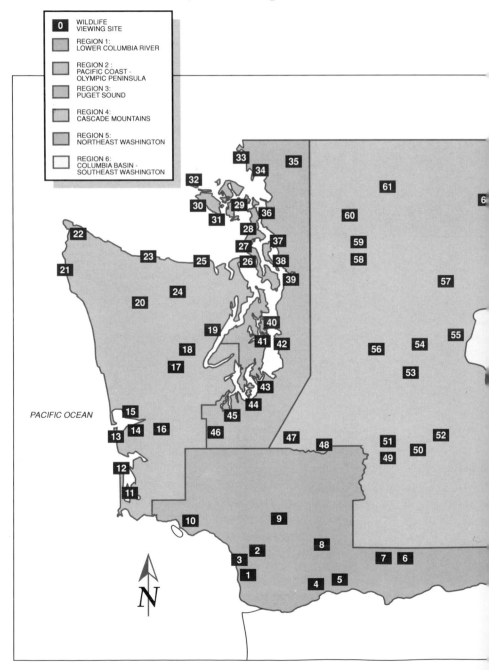

0	WILDLIFE VIEWING SITE
	REGION 1: LOWER COLUMBIA RIVER
	REGION 2: PACIFIC COAST - OLYMPIC PENINSULA
	REGION 3: PUGET SOUND
	REGION 4: CASCADE MOUNTAINS
	REGION 5: NORTHEAST WASHINGTON
	REGION 6: COLUMBIA BASIN - SOUTHEAST WASHINGTON

PACIFIC OCEAN

N

MAP INFORMATION

Washington's wildlife viewing sites have been organized into six viewing regions shown on this map. Within each region, sites are numbered consecutively in a general pattern. Each viewing region begins with a detailed map showing major roads and cities and the location of each wildlife viewing site.

HIGHWAY SIGNS

As you travel in Washington, look for these signs on interstates, highways, and other roads. They identify the route to follow to reach wildlife viewing sites.

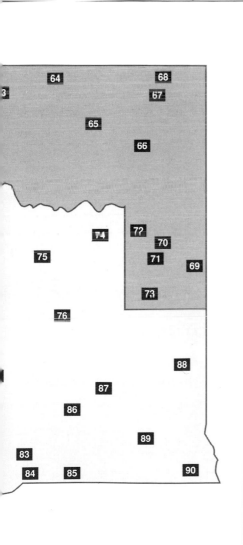

FEATURED WILDLIFE

 Songbirds, Perching Birds

Upland Birds

Shorebirds

 Raptors, Birds of Prey

 Marine Birds

 Wading Birds

 Waterfowl

Seals, Sea Lions, Otters

 Freshwater Mammals

 Whales, Dolphins

Fish

Hoofed Mammals

Carnivores Mammals

 Small Mammals

 Reptiles, Amphibians

 Tidepools

Wildflowers

FACILITIES AND RECREATION

P Parking

 Restrooms

Barrier-free

Hiking

Picinic

Camping

$ Entry Fee

Restaurant

 Small Boats

 Boat Ramp

 Large Boats

Bicycling

Cross-country Skiing

REGION 1: LOWER COLUMBIA RIVER

The Lower Columbia River region encompasses the southern Cascade Mountains, the narrow Columbia Gorge, and the broad, fertile floodplains of the lower Columbia River and its major tributaries. The Cascades are especially rugged in this region. The bottomlands of the Columbia and its major tributaries are characterized by stands of black cottonwood and other hardwood trees, and thousands of acres of freshwater marshes.

Wildlife of the region include the black-tailed deer, Roosevelt elk, and other species typical of the Cascade or Coast ranges. The endangered Columbian white-tailed deer is now restricted to narrow, wooded habitat along the lower Columbia River. Spring chinook and other races of Pacific salmon migrate upstream to spawn in the upper reaches of the Columbia and Snake river systems. Many thousands of ducks, geese, swans, and other migratory birds stop, rest, or winter in the productive bottomlands of the lower Columbia River region.

Photo, opposite page: Columbia River Gorge near Lyle, Washington. **BRUCE HANDS**

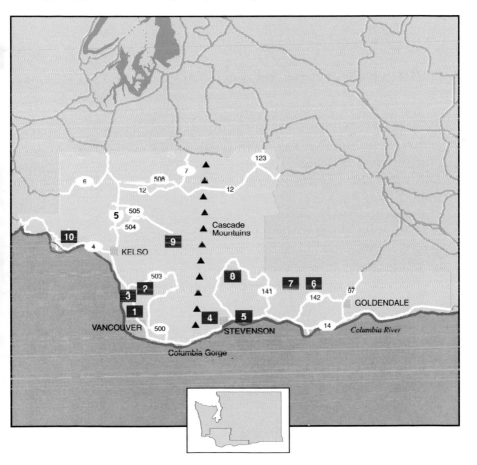

#		#	
1	Shillapoo and Post Office Lakes	6	Klickitat Wildlife Area
2	La Center Bottoms	7	Conboy Lake National Wildlife Refuge
3	Ridgefield National Wildlife Refuge	8	Lone Butte Wildlife Emphasis Area
4	Bonneville Dam	9	Mount St. Helens National Volcanic
5	Little White Salmon National Fish Hatchery		Monument
		10	Julia Butler Hansen National Wildlife Refuge

1 SHILLAPOO AND POST OFFICE LAKES

Description: Shillapoo and Post Office lakes are relicts of the natural flood-plain of the Columbia River.

Viewing Information: The entire Columbia River levee road (SR 501) is great for viewing wintering waterfowl and raptors. High probability of seeing large numbers of Canada geese, dabbling ducks, and tundra swans in winter and early spring. Good chance of seeing wintering bald eagles, ospreys, and other raptors. Moderate possibility of seeing sandhill cranes during fall migration. Spectacular views of four Cascade peaks. Boat ramp and trailhead at Shillapoo Lake. CHECK DATES OF FALL WATERFOWL HUNT AT SHILLAPOO LAKE.

Ownership: WDFW (360-696-6211); USFWS (360-887-4106)
Size: 241 acres (Shillapoo)
Closest Town: Vancouver, WA

2 LA CENTER BOTTOMS

Description: This bottomland along the East Fork of the Lewis River offers excellent bird watching near the town of La Center. Migrating Canada geese, tundra swans, and many ducks winter here. Bald eagles perch in trees above the river banks.

Viewing Information: High probability of viewing large numbers of Canada geese and ducks in fall and winter. Moderate probability of seeing tundra swans and bald eagles in winter. The town of La Center plans to develop a Watchable Wildlife site. Meanwhile, park on Fourth Street between Aspen and Birch avenues.

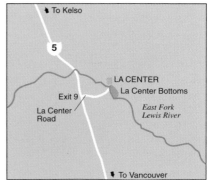

Ownership: PVT
Size: NA
Closest Town: La Center

16

3 RIDGEFIELD NATIONAL WILDLIFE REFUGE

Description: The lower Columbia River floodplain, with its mild, rainy winters and agricultural production, is a magnet for many thousands of wintering waterfowl on the Pacific Flyway. Ridgefield Refuge is a diverse community of sloughs, shallow ponds, and riparian woodlands. All seven subspecies of Canada geese found in the Pacific Flyway can be seen at Ridgefield, including the western Canada goose and the dusky, which nests in Alaska's Copper River Delta. Watch for tundra swans, bald eagles, and sandhill cranes. Black-tailed deer are common, and painted turtles are often seen basking on logs on sunny days.

Viewing Information: High probability of seeing large numbers of wintering ducks and Canada geese. Look for western Canada geese year-round. Good chance of seeing tundra swans in December through March, bald eagles in winter, and sandhill cranes during fall. Two main units of the refuge have been developed for public wildlife viewing, with ample parking and interpretive kiosks. At the Carty Unit, a two-mile self-guided "Oaks to Wetlands" interpretive trail winds through oak woodlands, wetlands, and open water habitats. Trailhead is one mile north of refuge headquarters in Ridgefield. The River "S" Unit features a maintained gravel road with designated parking areas and a wheelchair-accessible trail and observation blind at Rest Lake. Areas south and east of the road are closed to access from October 1-April 15. LIMITED-ENTRY HUNTING IS ALLOWED DURING FALL WATERFOWL SEASON IN THE AREA NORTH AND WEST OF THE RIVER "S" UNIT.

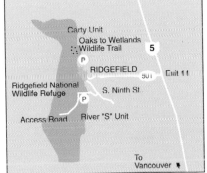

Ownership: USFWS (360-887-4106)
Size: 4,627 acres
Closest Town: Ridgefield

Sandhill cranes migrate through Washington each spring and fall on their way to and from breeding grounds in northern Canada, Alaska, and Siberia. During the breeding season, these birds perform a spectacular, elaborate mating dance. DEBI OTTINGER

17

LOWER COLUMBIA RIVER

4 BONNEVILLE DAM

Description: The Bonneville hydroelectric dam in the scenic Columbia River Gorge is one of the best sites in the Northwest for viewing annual salmon and steelhead trout runs. The dam includes fish ladders with viewing windows where visitors can watch fish pass as biologists count them. Salmon spawn in streams in Washington, Oregon, and Idaho. Some of these salmon stocks are in danger of extinction.

Viewing Information: Spring chinook salmon begin moving upriver in April. Other stocks of chinook, coho, and sockeye salmon and steelhead trout can be viewed from June through fall. Fall chinook runs peak in September. Visitor center is open daily until 5 p.m., with hours often extended to 8 p.m. in summer.

Ownership: ACE (503-374-8442)
Size: Ninety-seven acres
Closest Town: Stevenson

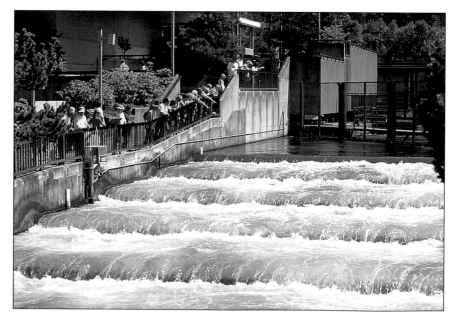

A 1988 survey found that 84% of Washington residents participated in some form of wildlife recreation. Wildlife photography and viewing alone contribute an estimated $1 billion each year to Washington's economy. BRUCE HANDS

5 LITTLE WHITE SALMON NATIONAL FISH HATCHERY

Description: Both chinook and coho salmon run up the Columbia River to this hatchery near the mouth of the Little White Salmon River in the Columbia Gorge. Waterfowl are seen along the river near the hatchery, as are osprey and bald eagles, which feed on spawned-out salmon carcasses. Other raptors, including golden eagles and an occasional peregrine falcon, may be seen in the Columbia Gorge. Wildflowers carpet the grassy slope above the river.

Viewing Information: Salmon can be seen spawning naturally downstream from the hatchery. They can also be seen year-round in rearing ponds. Visitor center is open during the spring chinook salmon run, which peaks in July, and during the longer fall chinook and coho salmon runs from September through November. Waterfowl and wildflowers are best in spring and summer. High probability of seeing bald eagles from December through March.

Ownership: USFWS (509-538-2755)
Size: 410 acres **Closest Town:** Stevenson

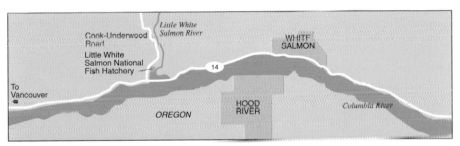

Fish ladders allow adult salmon, such as the coho shown here, to bypass dams during their upstream migration to spawning grounds. Certain races of Columbia River chinook salmon are nearing extinction. CHRIS HUSS

19

Washington Biodiversity:

The Life Cycle of the Pacific Salmon

Home can be many different places for migratory wildlife. Washington's rich biodiversity includes many animals found here only during one phase of their lives. The life cycle of the Pacific salmon is one of the most fascinating and dramatic examples of migratory wildlife in Washington. Five species and many races of Pacific salmon live in Washington waters. Some salmon never leave Puget Sound. Others spend years traveling in the North Pacific Ocean. All of these fish will eventually return to the stream where they were born in order to spawn, and then die. While it seems sad these magnificent fish must die, their bodies do not go to waste. Dead salmon are an important food source for wintering bald eagles and other animals. Their decomposing bodies add nutrients to the water.

The salmon's reproductive cycle usually begins in late summer or early fall, when adult fish migrate from saltwater to freshwater streams, a journey that may take weeks. Upon reaching their spawning grounds, the salmon release and fertilize eggs, covering them in a sand or gravel nest called a REDD. After about sixty days the eggs will hatch. The tiny salmon, called ALEVIN, develop in the redd until spring, when they emerge as FRY, and grow into SMOLTS. These young salmon are then ready to begin a long, often hazardous migration downstream to reach saltwater. Only about two percent of all salmon hatched will live to adulthood and go on to complete their role in this endless cycle of life and death.

6 KLICKITAT WILDLIFE AREA

Description: The vegetation and wildlife found here is typical of the eastern slopes of the southern Cascades: steep slopes, Ponderosa pine, and Oregon white oak, interspersed with open grassland.

Viewing Information: Managed primarily as wintering habitat for black-tailed deer; high probability of seeing deer on the Glenwood Highway (Leidl Grade) from January through March on south-facing slopes. Good chance of seeing mountain bluebirds and valley quail in spring, summer, and fall. Merriam's turkeys have been successfully introduced here. Although elusive, turkeys can be seen or heard in oak habitats in fall and spring (early morning hours are best). Both bald and golden eagles are commonly seen on Leidl Grade during winter months. The Klickitat River, which bisects the wildlife area, is one of the finest summer steelhead streams in the state. CHECK FALL DEER AND UP-LAND BIRD HUNTING SEASON. ALSO SPRING TURKEY SEASON FROM MID-APRIL TO MID-MAY.

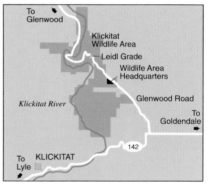

Ownership: WDFW (360-696-6211)
Size: 13,901 acres
Closest Town: Goldendale

Black bears inhabit the forested areas of all Washington mountain ranges. Although classified as carnivores, black bears more often eat roots, fruits, grasses, and insects.
TOM & PAT LEESON

7 CONBOY LAKE NATIONAL WILDLIFE REFUGE

Description: This large seasonal marsh at the base of 12,307-foot Mount Adams is a major stopover for migrating Canada geese, tundra swans, and many species of ducks, and the only known nesting location for sandhill cranes in Washington. Also watch for elk.

Viewing Information: High probability of seeing large numbers of geese, swans, and ducks in early spring. Moderate probability of seeing elk in spring and fall. Wildflowers abundant in spring. Headquarters six miles southwest of Glenwood. Public access limited to area around headquarters and Willard Springs Trail, and roadside viewing.

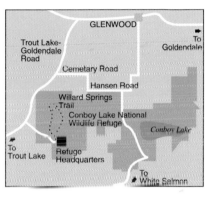

Ownership: USFWS (509-364-3410)
Size: 5,654 acres
Closest Town: Glenwood, White Salmon

8 LONE BUTTE WILDLIFE EMPHASIS AREA

Description: Wet and dry meadows and riparian corridors offer a diversity of habitats within the mixed conifer forest here. Residents include black-tailed deer, black bear, coyotes, beaver, and numerous songbirds. Good view of Mount Adams and other nearby peaks.

Viewing Information: Moderate probability of seeing deer and elk in summer and fall, especially in meadows. Low probability of seeing bear, coyotes, and beaver. Look for songbirds, wildflowers, and mushrooms in meadows during spring and summer. The management area is gated and interior roads are closed to motorized traffic. Pacific Crest Trail and Big Lava Beds nearby.

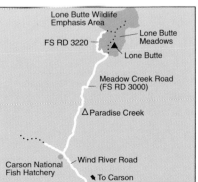

Ownership: USFS (509-395-2501)
Size: 12,450 acres
Closest Town: Carson, Cougar

23

9 MOUNT ST. HELENS NATIONAL VOLCANIC MONUMENT

Description: Mount St. Helens today is an excellent place to view wildlife of the southern Cascade Mountain Range, including black-tailed deer and the large Toutle elk herd. A variety of songbirds and pioneer plant species, including many wildflowers, are visible within the former blast zone.

Viewing Information: Mount St. Helens Visitor Center, five miles east of Castle Rock, is open daily from 9:00 a.m to 5:00 p.m. Trails, some wheelchair-accessible, are open to the public. A second visitor center will open at Coldwater Ridge, on the new Spirit Lake Highway (SR 504), in the fall of 1992. The new center will have spectacular views of the Toutle River Valley and Mount St. Helens lava dome. Look for deer and elk from SR 504 and other roads. Red-tailed hawks and other raptors can be seen in the rocks overlooking the highway and North Fork Toutle. Bald eagles winter along the lower Toutle River. The Toutle elk herd is often visible year-round with binoculars. Wildflowers are plentiful in the spring.

Ownership: USFS (360-247-5473); WDOT
Size: 110,000 acres   **Closest Town:** Castle Rock

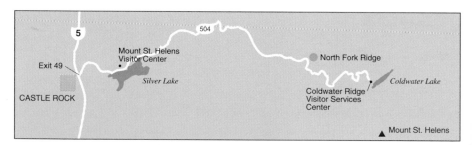

The eruption of Mount St. Helens on May 18, 1980, devastated plant and animal communities within the 150-square-mile blast zone. It was difficult to believe this area would ever support productive wildlife habitat again—but the natural healing process began almost immediately.
BRUCE HANDS

10 JULIA BUTLER HANSEN NATIONAL WILDLIFE REFUGE

Description: These woodlands and grasslands are intensively managed to protect an endangered subspecies, the Columbian white-tailed deer, which once roamed widely in the lower Columbia River drainage. Roosevelt elk from the surrounding Willapa Hills also forage here. Grasslands and shorelines on the refuge attract tundra swans, Canada geese, and other waterfowl and shorebirds. Watch for resident bald eagles, migratory warblers, and other songbirds.

Viewing Information: High probability of seeing deer and elk year-round, particularly from September to May in evening or early morning hours. Bald eagles are abundant in winter and nest here in spring. Warblers and songbirds are easily viewed during fall and spring migrations. Wildlife can be viewed from Brooks Slough and Steamboat Slough roads or by hiking the Center Road Trail from refuge headquarters.

Ownership: USFWS (360-795-3915)
Size: 4,400 acres
Closest Town: Cathlamet

Columbian white-tailed deer once ranged throughout the lower Columbia River and the Willamette River drainage of Oregon. Reported as common by Lewis and Clark in 1803, this subspecies is now endangered, found only on a few islands in the lower Columbia River and the Julia Butler Hansen National Wildlife Refuge in Washington.

DAVID MICHAEL JONES

25

REGION 2: PACIFIC COAST - OLYMPIC PENINSULA

The Pacific Coast-Olympic Peninsula region is known for its flat coastal plains, rugged seacoast, scenic mountain peaks, and the highest annual rainfall in the lower forty-eight states. The Olympic Mountain Range and the Willapa Hills to the south are fully exposed to the brunt of Pacific Ocean storms, resulting in lush forests of Douglas-fir, western hemlock, and western red cedar. The temperate rainforest on the west slope of the Olympics receives more than 100 inches of rainfall each year.

Wildlife identified with the region include Roosevelt elk, black bear, the northern spotted owl, the California gray whale, and thousands of ducks, geese, shorebirds and marine birds, which migrate along the Pacific Flyway to breed on offshore islands or feed in the large coastal estuaries of Grays Harbor and Willapa Bay.

Photo, opposite page: Ozette Islands, Olympic National Park. **ESTHER E. THOMPSON**

11	Willapa National Wildlife Refuge	20	Olympic National Park:
12	Leadbetter Point		Hoh Rainforest
13	Westport	21	Olympic National Park:
14	Johns River Wildlife Area		Ozette-Cape Alava
15	Grays Harbor National	22	Makah Bay and Cape Flattery
	Wildlife Refuge	23	Salt Creek Recreation Area
16	Friends Landing	24	Olympic National Park:
17	Brown Creek Nature Trail		Hurricane Ridge
18	Mount Ellinor Trail	25	Dungeness National Wildlife Refuge-
19	Duckabush Estuary		Recreation Area

11 WILLAPA NATIONAL WILDLIFE REFUGE

Description: This relatively unspoiled estuary supports a shellfish industry, a small fishing fleet, and a diversity of wildlife, including Roosevelt elk, black bear, and millions of migratory birds and waterfowl.

Viewing Information: There are five units of the refuge, each with different habitats and viewing opportunities. **Willapa Bay:** Vast beds of eelgrass and protected waters. High probability of seeing Canada geese and large numbers of ducks in late fall and winter. Good chance of seeing black brant, western sandpipers, Caspian terns, and other migratory birds in April and May. Best viewing near the refuge headquarters, the east shore of Long Island, and the north shore (off refuge) between Raymond and Tokeland. **Long Island:** Dense, rain-drenched coastal forest, surrounded by salt marsh and beach. Includes a 274-acre stand of old growth western red cedar. Deer, elk, black bear, and bald eagles might be seen on the island. Foot trails and five primitive campgrounds. ISLAND CAN BE REACHED ONLY BY SMALL BOAT. TIDES ARE TREACHEROUS. Ask at refuge headquarters for names of local for-hire boat operators. **Lewis Unit:** Large freshwater marsh near mouth of Bear River. Parking lot at trailhead. Good chance of seeing wintering trumpeter swans. Elk move down from Willapa Hills in winter and are visible on private land upstream from Highway 101; park off the road but PLEASE DO NOT TRESPASS ON PRIVATE LAND. **Riekkola Unit:** Diked grasslands managed for Canada geese, other waterfowl. Can be reached by road from Long Beach. CLOSED FROM OCTOBER 1-MARCH 31. **Leadbetter Point:** At the tip of the Long Beach Peninsula. See Site 12.

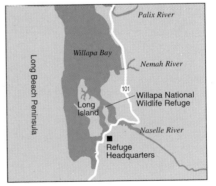

Ownership: USFWS (360-484-3482)
Size: 11,500 acres
Closest Town: Long Beach

Douglas-fir is dominant in many Pacific Northwest forests because of its tolerance to direct sunlight. Douglas-fir is not a true fir at all but has characteristics of both fir and hemlock trees.

⊗12 LEADBETTER POINT

Description: Surrounded by open water, these sand dunes, pine forest, and tidal marshes of Willapa Bay attract thousands of black brant that rest and feed here during their annual spring migration north to Alaska from wintering grounds in Mexico. Other waterfowl and shorebirds, including red knots and pectoral sandpipers, use the bay and interior dunes of the Long Beach Peninsula for cover and feeding during migration. On the ocean side, the rare snowy plover nests in small scrapes in the sand. Also watch for brown pelicans and, offshore, migrating gray whales in the spring.

Viewing Information: Fifteen miles north of the town of Long Beach. Good all-weather road. Parking and trailheads at Stackpole Slough and northern end of Leadbetter Point State Park. Short walk to the bay side of the spit, with high probability of seeing black brant and sandpipers in April and May. High probability of viewing trumpeter and tundra swans, and other waterfowl in late fall and winter. Trails to ocean beach offer moderate chance of seeing brown pelicans from June through September. Nesting snowy plovers can be viewed from a distance in spring. PARTS OF OCEAN BEACH ARE CLOSED FROM APRIL THROUGH AUGUST TO PROTECT NESTING SNOWY PLOVERS—PLEASE HEED CLOSURE SIGNS.

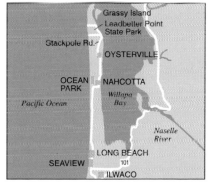

Ownership: USFWS (360-484-3482); WSP (360-642-3078)
Size: NA
Closest Town: Long Beach

The most abundant swan along the Pacific Flyway, tundra swans winter in Washington from mid-October through April. Most tundra swans breed in western Alaska, along the coast of the Bering Sea.

TOM & PAT LEESON

13 WESTPORT

Description: Westport is a bustling seaport town at the mouth of Grays Harbor. A municipal fishing pier, three large rock jetties, and two state park beaches offer good viewing of migrating gray whales, harbor seals, California sea lions, brown pelicans, Caspian terns, and other marine birds.

Viewing Information: Whale watching peaks during March, April, and May. Look for pelicans in summer. Arrange charter boat trips through Westport Chamber of Commerce. All species are also seen from ocean beaches and jetties. South Jetty has two observation towers.

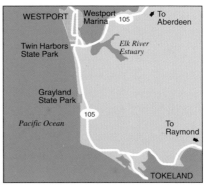

Ownership: Westport Chamber of Commerce (800-345-6223)
Size: NA
Closest Town: Westport

14 JOHNS RIVER WILDLIFE MANAGEMENT AREA

Description: This management area includes Markham Island and the mouth and four miles of the Johns River, providing cover and food for migratory birds and an expanding herd of Roosevelt elk. Also watch for raptors, including peregrine falcons, and black-tailed deer.

Viewing Information: Dike trails along Johns River extend into farm land and salt marsh. Good chance of seeing elk, deer, and waterfowl in fall and winter. BOATERS CHECK TIDE CHARTS—TIDES MAY EXCEED FOURTEEN FEET. AREA OPEN TO FALL HUNTING.

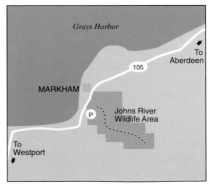

Ownership: WDFW (360-753-2600)
Size: 1,300 acres
Closest Town: Aberdeen

15 GRAYS HARBOR NATIONAL WILDLIFE REFUGE

Description: Over one million Western sandpipers and other shorebirds gather in Bowerman Basin to rest and feed on their annual spring migration between South America and the Arctic.

Viewing Information: This shorebird staging phenomenon lasts only a few days in the second half of April. When the birds arrive, the sky may be blocked out in places by the perfectly coordinated flying maneuvers of thousands of birds. Predators, including merlins and peregrine falcons, may also be viewed taking advantage of this avian smorgasbord. When the birds head north, viewing opportunities drop to a normal complement of local shorebirds, diving ducks, and great blue herons. Best viewing times are one hour before and after high tide. CHECK WITH THE REFUGE FOR OPTIMUM VIEWING DAYS AND TIDES. Parking is available at Bowerman Field Airport.

Ownership: USFWS (360-753-9467)
Size: Sixty-eight acres
Closest Town: Hoquiam

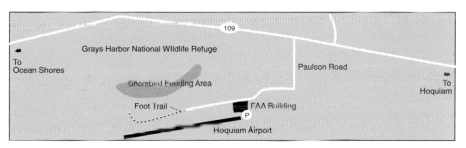

Commercial harvesting drove gray whales to the edge of extinction until the signing of an international treaty in 1946. Today, thousands of gray whales move along the Washington coast during their spring migration. RON SANFORD

16 FRIENDS LANDING

Description: The Grays Harbor Chapter of Trout Unlimited is developing this site to provide wildlife viewing and fishing for physically challenged visitors. An interpretive trail will loop around the thirty-two-acre pond and a fishing pier is being built. An old growth bottomland swamp harbors black-tailed deer and waterfowl. Residents include bald eagles and osprey.

Viewing Information: Site includes about a half-mile of river front along the Chehalis River. A bald eagle nest is visible from the pond. Ospreys are common on the lower Chehalis River.

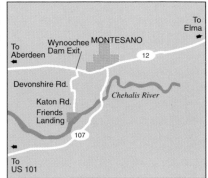

Ownership: PVT (Trout Unlimited) (360-533-4648)
Size: 152 acres
Closest Town: Montesano

17 BROWN CREEK NATURE TRAIL

Description: This hiking trail along the South Fork of the Skokomish River meanders through a beautiful grove of old growth Douglas fir. Beaver dams impound a small tributary to the South Fork, creating good habitat for wood ducks and forest songbirds. Watch for black-tailed deer.

Viewing Information: Beaver are nocturnal; watch for them in late afternoon or evening. Best chance of seeing black-tailed deer, wood ducks, and other waterfowl in spring and summer. Songbirds are common year-round. Roads are open year-round unless closed for snow. Trail is .8-mile long.

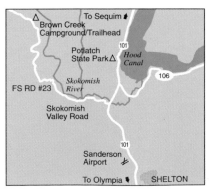

Ownership: USFS (360-877-5254)
Size: Ten acres (beaver ponds)
Closest Town: Hoodsport

18 MOUNT ELLINOR TRAIL

Description: Three miles of trails through second growth and old growth Douglas fir forest and a subalpine meadow lead to the summit of Mount Ellinor, the most accessible peak in the Olympic Mountains. At lower elevations, watch for Roosevelt elk and black-tailed deer; also ruffed grouse, gray jays, and songbirds. Cliffs are home to mountain goats.

Viewing Information: Good probability of seeing deer and elk. High probability of seeing mountain goats. Good spring and summer wildflowers in subalpine meadow. Excellent views of surrounding peaks and Puget Sound. UPPER ROADS ARE STEEP AND NARROW. USE TURNOUTS AND WATCH FOR LOGGING TRUCKS. TRAIL IS STEEP AND SLIPPERY.

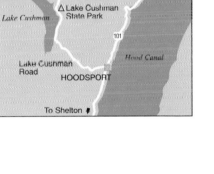

Ownership: USFS (360-877-5254)
Size: NA
Closest Town: Hoodsport

19 DUCKABUSH ESTUARY

Description: Hood Canal is the deepest, cleanest part of Puget Sound; estuaries here are highly productive habitats for fish and wildlife. Trumpeter swans, wigeon, pintails, and other waterfowl feed near shore. Harbor seals and bald eagles are also seen here.

Viewing Information: High probability of seeing large numbers of waterfowl in late fall and winter. Good probability of seeing bald eagles and trumpeter swans in winter. Look for harbor seals year-round. PLEASE DO NOT APPROACH OR DISTURB SEALS. Good viewing from Highway 101 with binoculars or a spotting scope. Roadside parking. USE CARE CROSSING THE HIGHWAY.

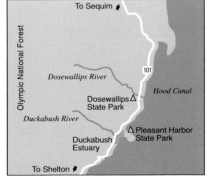

Ownership: PVT
Size: Approximately fifty acres
Closest Town: Brinnon

20 | OLYMPIC NATIONAL PARK: HOH RAINFOREST

Description: Temperate rainforests are found only in New Zealand, Chile, and here on the Olympic Peninsula, where the Hoh Valley receives an average of twelve feet of precipitation each year. Dense stands of old growth Sitka spruce and western hemlock filter rare sunlight to a muted shade of green. Sword ferns and hanging moss cling to trees, and sorrel carpets the forest floor. Douglas-fir and cedars reach world-record size in this cool, fog-bound "jungle." Native Roosevelt elk roam among the giant trees, as do black-tailed deer, black bear, bobcat, and mountain lions. Douglas squirrels scold hikers along nature trails. Along the Hoh's banks, look for river otters, spawning salmon, and harlequin ducks. The threatened and secretive spotted owl survives here.

Viewing Information: Elk move to higher elevations in summer, but other seasons find them just inside the park boundary and near Hoh campground and visitor center. Black bears may be encountered while camping, especially if food is not stored properly. Other predators are secretive; look for tracks on trails. Black-tailed deer are common; best chance to see river otters is early in the morning. WATCH FOR POISON OAK.

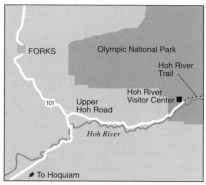

Ownership: NPS (360-374-6925 or 452-0330)
Size: Eighteen miles along the Hoh River
Closest Town: Forks

The temperate rainforest of Washington's north coast is known for heavy rainfall, summer fog, and huge bigleaf maple and other trees draped with lush clubmoss and licorice ferns.
CHARLES GURCHE

21 OLYMPIC NATIONAL PARK: OZETTE-CAPE ALAVA

Description: This remote ocean beach has productive tidepools, spectacular views of offshore islands, a large freshwater lake, and an abundance of wildlife. Black-tailed deer, including a population of albino deer, frequent the trails. Beach offers views of harbor seals, California sea lions, gray whales, and even sea otters floating in offshore kelp beds. Marine birds include tufted puffins and black oystercatchers. Bald eagles and osprey soar above the beach trails and around Lake Ozette.

Viewing Information: Two boardwalk trails from the Ozette Ranger Station to Cape Alava and Sand Point. High probability of seeing black tailed and albino deer on trails. Wildflowers, shorebirds, and waterfowl are common in the wet prairies. Good chance of seeing harbor seals, river otters, California sea lions, and many species of marine birds. Bald eagles and ospreys are common. Look for migrating California gray whales offshore in March, April, and May. Tidepools yield many small but unusual creatures at low tide, including hermit crabs, starfish, and sea anemones. Prehistoric Indian village site at Cape Alava. INCOMING TIDES ARE DANGEROUS; CHECK TIDE CHARTS. PLEASE DO NOT TOUCH OR DISTURB TIDE-POOL LIFE.

Ownership: NPS (360-452-0330)
Size: Trails: three miles to Sand Point and 3.3 mi. to Cape Alava
Closest Town: Sekiu

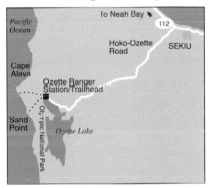

Olympic National Park hosts the largest unmanaged herd of Roosevelt elk in the nation. Roosevelt elk are close relatives of Rocky Mountain elk; the latter was reintroduced to eastern Washington in 1912.

J.C. MILLER

22 MAKAH BAY AND CAPE FLATTERY

Description: Located at the far northwest corner of the contiguous United States, this is one of the best places in Washington to observe sea otters, which feed in kelp beds. Seabirds fly between the cape and nearby Tatoosh Island. California gray whales swim offshore. Hobuck Beach offers tidepools and views of marine mammals, shorebirds, and migratory waterfowl, including trumpeter swans. Tidepools hold anemones, starfish, crabs, and shellfish.

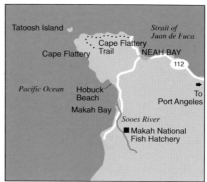

Viewing Information: Salmon run up the Sooes River to the Makah National Fish Hatchery. PLEASE RESPECT MAKAH INDIAN TRIBAL LAWS.

Ownership: Makah Indian Nation (360-645-2201); USFWS (360-645-2521)
Size: NA
Closest Town: Neah Bay

23 SALT CREEK RECREATION AREA

Description: This park boasts a large sandy beach, coastal rock formations, and some of the best tidepools in the state. At low tide, look for starfish, sea anemones, crabs, and other marine life. Rhinoceros auklets and other marine birds and waterfowl feed offshore. Black oystercatchers nest in rocks here. Bald eagles are seen year-round.

Viewing Information: Trails to Crescent Bay beach and tidepools begin at Salt Creek Park and at small satellite parking lot at Crescent Bay. Good chance of seeing auklets and other marine birds in spring, summer, and fall. Oystercatchers nest in spring and summer. PLEASE DO NOT TOUCH TIDEPOOL LIFE OR DISTURB NESTING BIRDS.

Ownership: Clallam County Parks
Size: 198 acres
Closest Town: Port Angeles

Washington Biodiversity:

Pacific Coast Migration Patterns

Washington's location on the North Pacific Ocean and its diversity of climatic conditions and habitats make the state an important place for migratory wildlife. In fact, many of Washington's most interesting and visible wildlife species move to, or through, Washington each year in search of food and breeding habitat.

California gray whales use the coastal waters of the Pacific Ocean as a marine "highway" connecting their summer feeding areas in the Arctic to their winter breeding grounds in Baja, California, Mexico.

Washington is also a critical component of the Pacific Flyway, the primary north-south migration route for millions of ducks, geese, swans, and shorebirds. These birds migrate each fall from nesting and rearing habitat in the north to winter feeding areas in the south, then north again in the spring. Many of these birds spend their winters in Washington, including snow geese, which migrate from Wrangel Island in distant Siberia.

Other species, including black brant and western sandpipers, depend on the state's coastal bays, estuaries, and freshwater wetlands as resting and feeding stops on their long migration from arctic breeding grounds to wintering areas as far away as South America. Many waterfowl species such as cinnamon teal descend on Washington's freshwater wetlands each year to nest and raise their young.

24 OLYMPIC NATIONAL PARK: HURRICANE RIDGE

Description: High meadows, glaciated peaks, and beautiful wildflowers give Hurricane Ridge an alpine quality, yet this is the most accessible area for visitors to experience the scenery and wildlife of the Olympic Mountain Range. Black-tailed deer and Olympic marmots frequent local trails; black bears forage here.

Viewing Information: From the main park visitor center in Port Angeles, a scenic parkway climbs steadily to the Hurricane Ridge Visitor Center, with interpretive programs, a sweeping view of the inner Olympic Range, and nearby access to Hurricane Hill and other trails. Road continues to Obstruction Point and other major trailheads. Wildflowers start blooming in early May and peak in mid-July. High probability of seeing black-tailed deer and Olympic marmots. Black bears are occasionally seen.

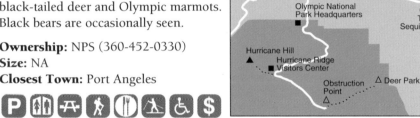

Ownership: NPS (360-452-0330)
Size: NA
Closest Town: Port Angeles

Male black-tailed deer shed their antlers each year. When new antlers begin to grow in early spring, they are covered with a soft, moss-like tissue called velvet. The velvet is rubbed off in time for the fall mating season, or "rut." ART WOLFE

25 DUNGENESS NATIONAL WILDLIFE REFUGE—RECREATION AREA

Description: Dungeness Spit is one of the longest natural sand spits in the world. Eelgrass beds in Dungeness Bay and the area inside the spit are protected from storms, attracting large concentrations of almost every waterfowl species that winters in western Washington, including harlequin ducks, scaup, and black brant. Shorebirds include plovers and dunlins. Harbor seals swim inside the spit and in the Strait of Juan de Fuca. Nearby Protection Island hosts a nesting colony of tufted puffins.

Viewing Information: Shorebirds can be seen in the fall and spring. Bald eagles are common in the winter, often roosting in trees overlooking the spit. Peregrine falcons seen occasionally. Harbor seals and pelagic marine birds are common year-round. Dungeness Refuge is a day-use area open only to foot traffic and horseback riding. Half-mile walk to an interpretive overlook above the spit and the Strait of Juan de Fuca. Raccoons often seen along this trail. The trail continues down a steep hill to the spit. Best viewing (and the least disturbing to wildlife) is within the first mile of Dungeness Spit. Dungeness Recreation Area, adjacent to the refuge, offers camping and hunting for waterfowl and pheasant during fall.

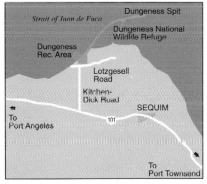

Ownership: USFWS (360-457-8451); Clallam County Parks (360-452-7831)
Size: Dungeness Spit is 5.5 miles long
Closest Town: Sequim

Tufted puffins nest in large colonies on rocky, offshore islands in Puget Sound and the Pacific Ocean. The bill of the puffin is well adapted to crush the shells of mollusks and sea urchins.
ART WOLFE

39

REGION 3: PUGET SOUND

When the last glaciers receded from Washington some 15,000 years ago, they left behind a deep inland sea, Puget Sound, which today is Washington's most unique and prominent natural feature. Wedged between the Olympic and Cascade mountain ranges, the Puget Sound basin is protected from the brunt of Pacific Ocean storms, giving it an ideal temperate climate. The Puget Sound region, with more than 1,000 miles of saltwater shoreline and many large islands, provides some of the most important wildlife habitat and best wildlife viewing opportunities in the western United States.

The waters and shoreline of Puget Sound make up a biologically-diverse ecosystem. The Sound is home to at least 211 species of marine fish, and a variety of marine birds, waterfowl, and marine mammals, including orca whales, California sea lions, and a large population of harbor seals. Rivers flowing into Puget Sound provide important migration corridors and spawning habitat for Pacific salmon. River estuaries are critical resting and feeding areas for ducks, geese, swans, and shorebirds migrating north and south along the Pacific Flyway.

Photo, opposite page: San Juan Islands, Puget Sound.
SCOTT SPIKER

26	Keystone Ferry
27	Joseph Whidbey State Park
28	Deception Pass State Park
29	San Juan Ferry
30	San Juan Island: Lime Kiln Point State Park
31	San Juan Island: Cattle Point
32	Stuart Island: Turn Point
33	Birch Bay State Park
34	Tennant Lake Interpretive Center
35	North Fork Nooksack River
36	Padilla Bay National Estuarine Research Reserve
37	Skagit Wildlife Area
38	Kayak Point Regional Park
39	Langus Riverfront Park and Nature Trail
40	Hiram M. Chittenden Locks
41	Fort Ward State Park
42	Mercer Slough Nature Park
43	The Nature Center At Snake Lake
44	Nisqually National Wildlife Refuge
45	Tumwater Falls Park
46	Mima Mounds Natural Area Preserve

26 KEYSTONE FERRY

Description: The ferry ride across turbulent Admiralty Inlet, from Port Townsend to Whidbey Island, offers a good opportunity to see marine birds and mammals. Watch for small pods of orcas (killer whales). Dall's porpoises often play in the bow waves of ferries and other vessels. Marine birds, including rhinoceros auklets and pigeon guillemots, are common in mid-channel. Harbor seals are seen around the ferry docks at both ends of the route.

Viewing Information: Moderate probability of seeing orcas in summer. Marine birds are best viewed in summer; seals year-round.

Ownership: WDOT (800-84-FERRY)
Size: Four-mile ferry route
Closest Town: Port Townsend

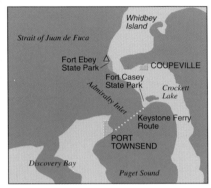

27 JOSEPH WHIDBEY STATE PARK

Description: This small day-use park is one of the best places on Whidbey Island to observe waterfowl, marine birds, and other wildlife. A half-mile trail through a freshwater wetland offers good views of migrating and nesting waterfowl and marsh birds. Pigeon guillemots, black oystercatchers, tufted puffins, and pelagic cormorants nest on Smith Island, seven miles offshore. These birds, along with rhinoceros auklets, harlequin ducks, and black brant, frequent the channel and feed near shore.

Viewing Information: High probability of seeing waterfowl and marine birds year-round. Watch for orcas from the beach in summer. Parking lot is sometimes closed in winter; park and beach are open to foot traffic year-round.

Ownership: WSP (360-678-4636)
Size: 112 acres
Closest Town: Oak Harbor

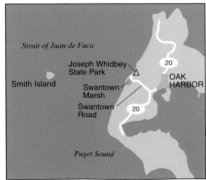

Description: This scenic park of old growth Douglas-fir forest, saltwater beaches, tidepools, and freshwater lakes and marshes straddles the narrow, rocky channel between Whidbey Island and Fidalgo Island in northern Puget Sound. Black-tailed deer are common. Bald eagles perch in tall trees and soar overhead, and a variety of marine birds and waterfowl raft offshore or rest on the lakes and quiet bays.

Viewing Information: Cranberry Lake, on Whidbey Island, is a good place to see loons, grebes, and resting waterfowl. Marbled murrelets and other marine birds can be viewed from the West Beach sand dune trail west of Cranberry Lake. The area around Cornet Bay, on the east side of Highway 20, has an osprey nest and foot trails through mature Douglas-fir forest. The area facing Puget Sound on the north side of Deception Pass offers panoramic views of the Olympic Mountains and nearby San Juan Islands. Orcas and other marine mammals can sometimes be observed traversing Rosario Strait. Most heavily visited state park. Due to high summer visitation, wildlife viewing is best in early morning, evening, and off-season.

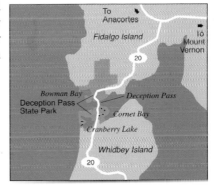

Ownership: WSP (360-675-2417)
Size: 3,133 acres
Closest Town: Oak Harbor

Red and purple sea urchins live in deeper tidepools, where they are covered by seawater during all but the lowest of tides. Sea urchins feed on drifting pieces of kelp and other algae.
PAT O'HARA

29 SAN JUAN FERRY

Description: The scenic ferry ride from Anacortes through the San Juan Islands offers some of the most beautiful scenery and best marine wildlife viewing opportunities in Puget Sound. The San Juans consist of 468 islands and protruding rocks in northern Puget Sound; eighty-four islands are included in the San Juan National Wildlife Refuge. The islands receive less rain than coastal areas due to the rainshadow effect of the Olympic Mountains. This drier climate, along with the strategic location of the islands in the migratory path of many bird and marine mammal species, results in many unique viewing opportunities. The San Juans support the largest year-round population of bald eagles in the lower United States. Golden eagles, more typical of arid eastern Washington, also live here. Many smaller islands support breeding populations of tufted puffins and rhinoceros auklets. Orcas (killer whales), minke whales, Dall's porpoises, sea lions, and harbor seals also ply these waters.

Viewing Information: The San Juan Ferry winds through some outstanding wildlife viewing locations. The ferry leaves Anacortes heading west, then crosses Rosario Strait, where rafts of scoters, rhinoceros auklets, and other marine birds often ride the water. Smith Island to the south is a major breeding area for tufted puffins and auklets. Rosario Strait is a major thoroughfare for orcas and minke whales, especially between May and September. After crossing Rosario Strait, the ferry navigates Thatcher Pass between Blakely and Decatur islands. Look for California sea lions and harbor seals, which haul out on rocks and isolated beaches. Bald eagles nest on Humphrey Head, on the north end of Lopez Island. Eagles can be seen near all islands, perched in treetops or soaring overhead. Turkey vultures circle the islands on warm afternoons. Disembark at Friday Harbor to visit sites 30 and 31. Ferry continues to Sidney, B. C., with additional viewing opportunities. SUMMER AUTOMOBILE TRAFFIC IS HEAVY BUT THERE IS ALWAYS ROOM FOR WALK-ON PASSENGERS.

Ownership: WDOT (800-84-FERRY)
Size: NA
Closest Town: Anacortes, Friday Harbor, Sidney

30 | SAN JUAN ISLAND: LIME KILN POINT STATE PARK

Description: Lime Kiln Point is one of the most reliable places to see orcas (killer whales), minke whales, and Dall's porpoises. There are three resident pods, or packs, of orcas, totalling about ninety animals, in the greater Puget Sound area, plus transient pods from Pacific Ocean and Canadian waters. Orcas congregate here in summer to feed on salmon moving into freshwater streams to spawn. Minke whales, the smallest of the baleen family, are also observed here. Minkes usually travel alone and are more difficult to spot with their low profile and small dorsal fin. Dall's porpoises, harbor porpoises, river otters, bald eagles, and marine birds also pass Lime Kiln Point.

Viewing Information: Moderate probability of seeing orcas, often daily, between May and September. The large black dorsal fin is visible from far off. A loud exhaling sound is often heard even before the whales surface. Orcas are seldom sighted in winter. Look for minke whales in summer. VEGETATION IS FRAGILE; PLEASE STAY ON TRAILS. The Whale Museum in Friday Harbor offers excellent exhibits; open daily.

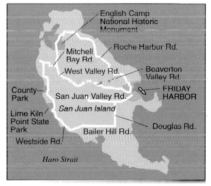

Ownership: WSP (360-378-2044)
Size: Thirty-nine acres
Closest Town: Friday Harbor

Scientists have divided orcas in British Columbia and Washington waters into three distinct pods, or communities, each with its own "language," feeding habits, and social behavior. LEE MANN

31 SAN JUAN ISLAND: CATTLE POINT

Description: This rocky, windswept point is one of the best places in the San Juans to view bald and sometimes golden eagles. The point provides a panoramic view of wildlife moving through the narrow channel between San Juan and Lopez islands. Offshore islands attract breeding colonies of gulls—sometimes harassed by eagles feeding on young birds. Also watch for marine birds, orca and minke whales, and harbor seals.

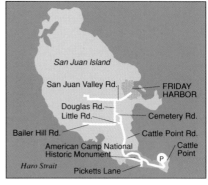

Viewing Information: Bald eagles and other species are present year-round. Eagles often roost in nearby trees and soar overhead.

Ownership: WDNR (360-856-3500)
Size: Approximately ten acres
Closest Town: Friday Harbor

32 STUART ISLAND: TURN POINT

Description: Turn Point, at the north tip of Stuart Island in the San Juans, offers excellent viewing of orcas, minke whales, bald eagles, and marine birds. The site includes a lighthouse and is a good vantage for watching ships moving to and from the port of Vancouver, B.C.

Viewing Information: Bald eagles nest and roost in nearby trees. Orcas may be seen between May and September, sometimes feeding close to shore. Minke whales may appear between Stuart and Waldron islands during summer migration. Stuart Island can be reached only by private boat or airplane. Camping and mooring facilities at nearby Stuart Island State Park only.

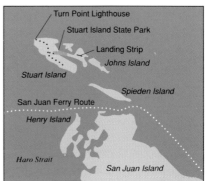

Ownership: BLM (360-662-4223)
Size: Sixty-eight acres
Closest Town: Friday Harbor (San Juan Island)

33 BIRCH BAY STATE PARK

Description: This large, shallow, protected saltwater bay has more than two miles of saltwater shoreline. Rich eelgrass beds attract large numbers of waterfowl and wading birds during low tides. More than 100 species of birds are seen here, including harlequin ducks and bald eagles. Large flocks of black brant rest here on their long migration north. Just east of the park, on private land, is one of the largest great blue heron rookeries in the state. Herons from this rookery often feed in groups of a dozen or more on outgoing tides.

Viewing Information: Good chance of seeing wintering bald eagles and, occasionally, peregrine falcons pursuing shorebirds. Black brant pause here in April. The Terrell Marsh Trail goes from the campground, through mixed Douglas-fir and birch forest, to a freshwater marsh, where waterfowl and marsh birds may be observed. With its sandy bottom and clean, shallow water, Birch Bay is popular for clamming and beachcombing.

Ownership: WSP (360-371-2800)
Size: 193 acres
Closest Town: Blaine

Wintering along the Pacific coast, harlequin ducks migrate inland each spring to nest and raise their young on lakes and streams in the Olympics, Cascades, and other Washington mountain ranges.
ART WOLFE

34 | TENNANT LAKE INTERPRETIVE CENTER

Description: URBAN SITE. Tennant Lake harbors dabbling and diving ducks, bald eagles, Cooper's hawks, and rough-legged hawks. Canada geese, wood ducks, and other waterfowl nest and raise their young here. Green-backed and great blue herons, and other wading and shorebirds are also common.

Viewing Information: High probability of seeing ducks and raptors in fall, winter, and early spring. High probability of seeing Canada geese and wood ducks in spring and summer. Part of Hovander Homestead Park, which includes a barrier-free, braille-signed "fragrance garden." Interpretive center has an observation tower and a boardwalk through the swamp to the lake.

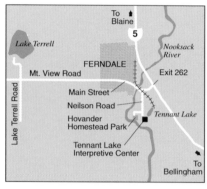

Ownership: Whatcom County Parks (360-384-3444)
Size: 720 acres
Closest Town: Ferndale

35 | NORTH FORK NOOKSACK RIVER

Description: The North Fork of the Nooksack River hosts one the largest and most visible concentrations of wintering bald eagles in the lower United States.

Viewing Information: Migration coincides with fall-winter spawning run of chum salmon. Eagles arrive as early as October; peak concentration (100 or more eagles) occurs in December or early January. Wintering eagles leave by March. Best viewing is at the Nooksack Salmon Hatchery, one mile south of Kendall, or the Welcome Bridge on Mosquito Lake Road, five miles south of the hatchery. Elk winter in fields near the Welcome Bridge. DO NOT PARK IN FRONT OF THE WELCOME FIRE STATION.

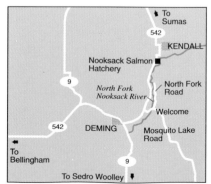

Ownership: WDFW (360-428-1520); PVT
Size: Ten miles Kendall to Deming
Closest Town: Kendall

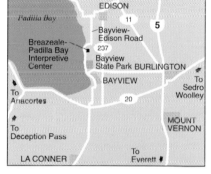

Description: This pristine estuary, with its extensive tidal flats and eelgrass beds, is one of the best places in Puget Sound to view marine birds, waterfowl, shorebirds, and birds of prey. The estuary attracts many waterfowl species, including canvasbacks, harlequin ducks, and black brant, a small marine goose that nests in the Arctic. Harbor seals are common in the bay as are great blue herons, dunlins, and black-bellied plovers. Migrating peregrine falcons feed on shorebirds. Bald eagles nest nearby.

Viewing Information: A high observation deck and a special viewing blind (open November–March) offer expansive views of the bay and its wildlife. The Breazeale-Padilla Bay Interpretive Center includes interpretive exhibits, indoor aquariums, a theater, and a "hands-on" room where visitors can touch and closely look at features of this estuarine environment. From the interpretive center, visitors may take a mile-long upland trail or a short trail to the beach. A 2.25-mile interpretive trail along the dike at the south end of the bay provides views of the high intertidal area and brackish sloughs. High to moderate probability of seeing eagles year-round. Low probability of seeing peregrine falcons in fall and winter. Interpretive center open from 10:00 a.m. to 5:00 p.m. every day except Monday and Tuesday.

Ownership: WDOE (360-428-1558)
Size: 2,600 acres
Closest Town: Burlington

The low marsh vegetation of the Skagit and Stillaguamish river deltas is ideal habitat for wintering snow geese; a large percentage of the Pacific Coast population of lesser snow geese winters in these Puget Sound estuaries each year.
LEE MANN

49

37 SKAGIT WILDLIFE AREA

Description: The Skagit River delta on Puget Sound is one of the most important and productive waterfowl wintering areas in the western arm of the Pacific Flyway. The area is famous for its wintering population of lesser snow geese, which migrate here from Wrangell Island in Siberia. Most of the estuary is included in the Skagit Wildlife Area, which is diked, farmed, and intensively managed for waterfowl and shorebirds. As many as 300 tundra swans winter here. More than 125,000 ducks, including mallards, teal, wigeon, and pintails, have been seen on Skagit Bay during the winter peak. Bald eagles and peregrine falcons feed here, along with northern harriers and red-tailed hawks. Black-tailed deer, beaver, and river otters inhabit the sloughs and channels.

Viewing Information: Up to 27,000 snow geese arrive in late fall and usually stay through April. High probability of seeing other waterfowl in spring, fall, and winter. Moderate probability of seeing raptors in winter. From Conway, drive to the Skagit Wildlife Area headquarters, where trail and viewing information is available. A two-mile loop trail on the dikes allows viewing of snow geese and other waterfowl. Other good viewing areas include the end of Fir Island (Maupin) Road and the end of Rawlins Road on the North Fork Skagit. SKAGIT WILDLIFE AREA IS OPEN FOR HUNTING DURING FALL WATERFOWL SEASON.

Ownership: WDW (360-775-1311)
Size: 12,000 acres
Closest Town: Mount Vernon

The snowy owl is an irregular winter visitor to Washington. The abundance of this large, white raptor is keyed to the availability of small rodent populations in its Arctic breeding range.
GORDON SULLIVAN

38 KAYAK POINT REGIONAL PARK

Description: Port Susan Bay is one of the most productive estuaries in Puget Sound, attracting waterfowl and large numbers of marine birds. Kayak Point, on the east side of the bay, offers excellent year-round wildlife viewing. From the 300-foot fishing pier, watch for snow geese, black brant, ducks, loons, and grebes. California gray whales sometimes come within 100 feet of the pier; sea lions also swim here. Bald eagles nest and roost in nearby trees.

Viewing Information: High probability of seeing waterfowl and marine birds in fall, winter, and spring. Look for sea lions in winter and early spring; gray whales April through June. Trails lead from campground to cliffs and beaches.

Ownership: Snohomish County Parks (360-388-3415)
Size: 670 acres
Closest Town: Marysville

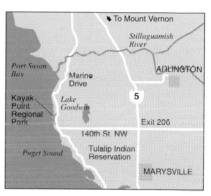

39 LANGUS RIVERFRONT PARK AND NATURE TRAIL

Description: URBAN SITE. This walking trail winds along Union Slough and the lower Snohomish River, one of Puget Sound's largest estuaries. The trail passes through stands of cottonwood and alder, wetlands, and former farmland on the floodplain. A variety of songbirds, including red-winged blackbirds, nest in wetlands. Bald eagles and other raptors perch in trees along river channels.

Viewing Information: High probability of seeing waterfowl, raptors, and shorebirds year-round. Future development will include an interpretive center and wildlife viewing platform.

Ownership: City of Everett Parks and Recreation (425-259-0300)
Size: 2.75-mile trail
Closest Town: Everett

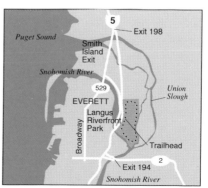

40 HIRAM M. CHITTENDEN LOCKS

Description: URBAN SITE. The Chittenden (Ballard) Locks in Seattle are the key navigational link between the saltwater environment of Puget Sound and the Lake Washington Ship Canal. A botanical garden and many large trees attract a variety of songbirds and eastern gray squirrels. Great blue herons and bald eagles feed here on migrating salmon and steelhead trout, as do a number of voracious California sea lions (collectively known as "Herschel").

Viewing Information: Sea lions are common from September through early summer. Sockeye run starts in June and July; chinook and coho in September and October; steelhead in late fall and winter. Locks include a fish ladder and underwater fish viewing room.

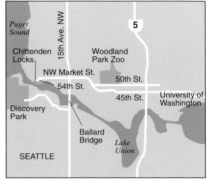

Ownership: ACE (206-783-7001)
Size: Seventeen acres
Closest Town: Seattle

41 FORT WARD STATE PARK

Description: Fort Ward State Park, at the south end of Bainbridge Island, is a short ferry ride from Seattle and offers views of marine birds and mammals. Douglas squirrels, Steller's jays, and other small wildlife are seen along the wooded trail from the picnic area to the beach. Black-tailed deer are common but elusive. Bald eagles occasionally roost here.

Viewing Information: Viewing is best during fall, winter, and spring. Two blinds on the beach provide good viewing of marine birds, shorebirds, and waterfowl on Rich Passage.

Ownership: WSP (206-842-3931)
Size: 137 acres
Closest Town: Winslow

42 MERCER SLOUGH NATURE PARK

Description: URBAN SITE. Boardwalks and trails offer a quiet sanctuary and good viewing of goldeneyes, ruddy ducks, mallards, Canada geese, and pied-billed grebes. Marsh residents include beaver, muskrats, and river otter. Coyotes sometimes wail at the sirens of emergency vehicles on Bellevue Way. Red-tailed hawks perch on power poles.

Viewing Information: Waterfowl and shorebirds are seen year-round. Look for goldeneyes and ruddy ducks in winter; nesting mallards, Canada geese, and pied-billed grebes in spring. Summer is best for beaver, muskrats, and river otter. Good canoeing; put-ins at Enatai Beach and Sweyolocken Park.

Ownership: City of Bellevue Parks and Recreation (206-455-6885)
Size: 320 acres
Closest Town: Bellevue

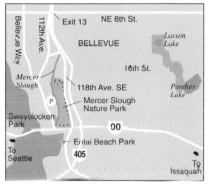

43 THE NATURE CENTER AT SNAKE LAKE

Description: URBAN SITE. A haven for wildlife in the heart of Tacoma. The Nature Center includes two miles of self-guided trails with four observation shelters. Trails wind through Douglas-fir forest, meadows, and wetlands. Snake Lake attracts many songbirds, including towhees, kinglets, and cedar waxwings. Canada geese, wood ducks, and great blue herons are common. Watch for red fox, and raccoons.

Viewing Information: High probability of seeing waterfowl and great blue herons year-round. Red fox and raccoons are best seen in early morning or evening. Nature center and trails open daily 8:00 a.m. until dusk.

Ownership: Metropolitan Park District of Tacoma (253-591-6439)
Size: Fifty-four acres
Closest Town: Tacoma

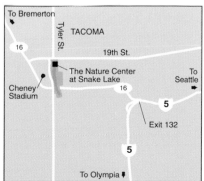

44 NISQUALLY NATIONAL WILDLIFE REFUGE

Description: This refuge was established in 1974 to protect the Nisqually Delta, one of the largest remaining undeveloped estuaries in Washington. Nisqually Refuge is a scenic and biological oasis on the Interstate 5 corridor. During fall and winter migration, up to 20,000 wigeon, mallards, teal, and other ducks gather here. Bald eagles nest on-site; other raptors are common.

Viewing Information: Viewing is good year-round, particularly for songbirds, herons, and other wading birds. The refuge is open year-round and wildlife viewing is encouraged, although jogging, pets, bicycling, and other activities considered disturbing to wildlife are discouraged. The refuge includes three loop trails of half-mile, one-mile, and 5.5-mile lengths with access to observation decks, photo blinds, and the Twin Barns Education Center, open on weekends. Luhr Beach has a boat ramp. Hunting is allowed on state-owned lands adjacent to the refuge. STRONG TIDES. CHECK TIDE TABLE BEFORE ENTERING REFUGE BY BOAT.

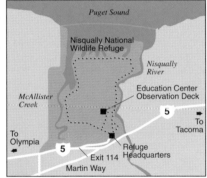

Ownership: USFWS (360-753-9467)
Size: 2,818 acres
Closest Town: Olympia

The large, conical bill of the evening grosbeak enables it to crack very hard seeds, including those of vine maple, hemlock, and mountain ash. Common in coniferous forests of the Cascade Mountains, grosbeaks are often seen in cities and suburban neighborhoods around Puget Sound in the fall and winter.
RON SPOMER

45 TUMWATER FALLS PARK

Description: URBAN SITE. Thousands of chinook and coho salmon struggle to pass Tumwater Falls on their annual spawning run up the Deschutes River. Each year up to 6,000 adult coho salmon use fish ladders to bypass the falls. The Washington Department of Fisheries collects 5,000 to 20,000 returning chinook, holding them in two ponds located in the park.

Viewing Information: Every Monday, Wednesday, and Friday from mid-September to early November, visitors can watch as hatchery workers collect eggs from the female fish. In spring, finger-lings are released in the Deschutes River. A trail along the river offers year-round viewing of waterfowl and songbirds. Open daily from 8:00 a.m. to dusk.

Ownership: PVT (Olympia-Tumwater Foundation); WDF (360 753 6600)
Size: NA
Closest Town: Olympia, Tumwater

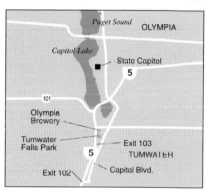

46 MIMA MOUNDS NATURAL AREA PRESERVE

Description: The Mima Prairie is covered with hundreds of circular earth mounds, some more than six feet tall and thirty feet across. These mounds have been studied by scientists for more than a century but their origin is still a mystery. Two theories are that the mounds were created by receding glaciers, or built by giant pocket gophers!

Viewing Information: The preserve is open year-round during daylight hours. A half-mile nature trail winds through the mounds; other trails extend into the preserve. Songbirds are common and wildflower displays are outstanding in spring and summer. Trails are closed to horses and motor vehicles.

Ownership: WDNR (360-748-2383)
Size: 445 acres
Closest Town: Littlerock

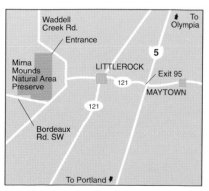

REGION 4: CASCADE MOUNTAINS

The Cascade Mountain Range is the backbone of Washington, bisecting the state into the moist, densely-forested regions of the Pacific Coast and Puget Sound, and the high desert country of eastern Washington. Cascade Mountain peaks soar to an average height of 6,000 to 8,000 feet; Mount Rainier, at 14,410 feet, is the spectacular crown of this range. The west slope of the Cascades is characterized by dense forests of Douglas-fir and western hemlock. The east slope, in the rainshadow of Pacific Ocean storms, is known for dry Ponderosa pine forests, native shrub-steppe vegetation, and basaltic rock formations.

Wildlife of the Cascade Mountains is magnificent and diverse. The west slope is known for large populations of black-tailed deer, and other forest-dependent mammals and bird species. The eastern slope, steeper and much more open, is home to Rocky Mountain elk, mule deer, and many transitional species found in both mountainous and high desert ecosystems.

Photo, opposite page: Mount Shuksan and Picture Lake, North Cascades National Park. ESTHER E. THOMPSON

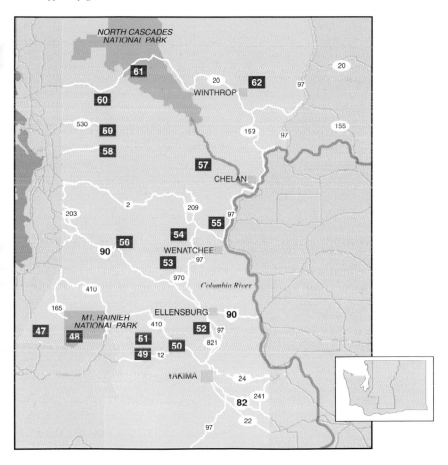

#		#	
47	Northwest Trek Wildlife Park	55	Swakane Canyon
48	Mount Rainier National Park	56	Gold Creek Pond
49	Rimrock Lake and Clear Lake	57	Lake Chelan
50	Oak Creek Wildlife Area	58	Mountain Loop Highway
51	Timberwolf Mountain	59	Fortson Mill Ponds
52	Yakima River Canyon	60	Upper Skagit Bald Eagle Area
53	Red Top Mountain	61	North Cascades Highway
54	Icicle Creek Canyon	62	Methow Wildlife Area

47 NORTHWEST TREK WILDLIFE PARK

Description: Northwest Trek is a large, open-air zoological park in the Cascade foothills near Mount Rainier. The zoo emphasizes educating the public, especially children, about native wildlife. A 435-acre enclosure allows Roosevelt elk, woodland caribou, and other wildlife to roam freely.

Viewing Information: The park is open daily from mid-February through October; Friday through Sunday and selected holidays the rest of the year. Visitor center includes a gift shop, cafe, the Forest Theater, and the Cheney Discovery Center of hands-on educational displays. Five miles of trails; tour tram through the 435-acre enclosure.

Ownership: Metropolitan Park District of Tacoma (253-832-6117); Recorded information: 800-433-TREK
Size: 635 acres
Closest Town: Eatonville

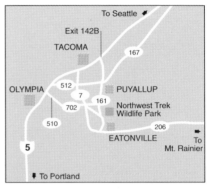

Solitary and secretive by nature, cougars prey almost exclusively on deer and small mammals. Cougars are found throughout Washington's forested mountains but are seldom seen by humans. DARRELL GULIN

Description: Mount Rainier, at 14,410 feet, dominates the Cascade Range and surrounding landscape for 100 miles around. Higher elevations are encased in permanent snowpack and glaciers, but the park contains a wide diversity of wildlife habitats, from subalpine meadows to streamside corridors and low-elevation old growth forests.

Viewing Information: Wildlife viewing opportunities depend on the time of year, the location within the park, and, to a very large degree, the number of people using the campgrounds, trails, and internal road system. There are more than 300 miles of trails, and four visitor centers—at Longmire, Paradise, Ohanapecosh, and Sunrise. Each visitor center has information on nearby trails, habitats, and associated wildlife. Mount Rainier is famous for high-meadow wildflowers that begin with snow melt in mid-June and peak in late July and August. Mountain goats are native here and can be viewed at higher elevations, including Backbone Ridge and Goat Island Mountain, visible from the Sunrise Visitor Center. Black-tailed deer are common in all forested areas of the park. Elk spend summers at higher elevations, then move downstream to winter along forested river bottoms; elk are best seen during these spring and fall vertical migrations. Almost any wildlife species native to the Cascades can be encountered in this huge, protected park, but the casual visitor is most likely to see deer and a variety of mountain songbirds and small mammals such as chipmunks, Douglas squirrels, and hoary marmots.

Ownership: NPS (360-569-2211)
Size: 235,612 acres
Closest Town: Packwood, Buckley

The mountain goat is not a true goat—it is a mountain-dwelling antelope. Mountain goats are native to the Cascade and Selkirk mountain ranges of Washington. They were also introduced to Olympic National Park in the 1920's.
RON SPOMER

49 RIMROCK LAKE AND CLEAR LAKE

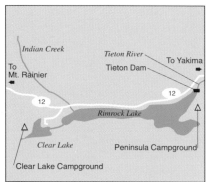

Description: Rimrock and Clear lakes pack a variety of good wildlife viewing opportunities into a small area. Bald eagles regularly nest near Tieton Dam and the Peninsula Campground. Ospreys and nesting waterfowl also frequent the lakes. The North Fork Tieton River, between the two lakes, is an excellent place to view spawning kokanee, a small landlocked variety of sockeye salmon. Fish can be viewed from bridges in Clear Lake Campground, from the river bank, or along Indian Creek, upstream from Rimrock Lake. Rocky Mountain elk roam the forest around the lakes.

Viewing Information: Located on the scenic White Pass Highway near the crest of the Cascades. Moderate to high probability of seeing eagles in spring and summer. Look for osprey and waterfowl from spring into fall. Elk are most often seen in fall. A barrier-free nature trail with wildlife viewing blinds is being constructed on the west side of Clear Lake.

Ownership: USFS (509-653-2205)
Size: 345 acres
Closest Town: Naches

Kokanee, a land-locked variety of sockeye salmon, occur naturally in Washington's many deep, cool lakes. Like their sea-running relatives, kokanee move out of deep water each fall to spawn in tributary streams. GARY BRAASCH

Description: Oak Creek is managed as wintering habitat for the Yakima herd of Rocky Mountain elk; visitors can observe hundreds of elk up-close at feeding stations. Steep hillsides, basaltic rock formations, and wooded oak canyons also provide transitional habitat for mountain and shrub-steppe desert wildlife. Watch for golden eagles, prairie falcons, and other raptors. Lewis' woodpeckers, western tanagers, and other songbirds frequent the wooded draws. The western gray squirrel, uncommon in Washington, lives along Oak Creek and other drainages. A small population of California bighorn sheep may often be seen at a winter feeding station at the foot of nearby Clemens Mountain.

Viewing Information: The number of visible elk and the duration of supplemental feeding varies annually, but winter viewing is usually good at feeding stations near the junction of Highways 12 and 410. Moderate to high probability of seeing raptors, songbirds, and gray squirrels spring and summer.

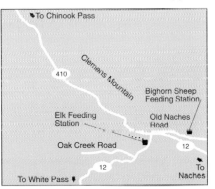

Ownership: WDFW (509-575-2740)
Size: 84,000 acres
Closest Town: Naches

The Yakima elk herd has traditionally migrated from higher elevations on the east slope of the Cascade Mountains to winter in the foothills of the Yakima Valley. As apple orchards and residential neighborhoods gradually replaced traditional wintering areas, it has become necessary to feed large numbers of elk in the winter to ensure their survival. CURT GIVEN

51 TIMBERWOLF MOUNTAIN

Description: This former fire lookout offers panoramic views of the east slope of the Cascades. Spruce forest, subalpine meadows, and wooded draws dominated by aspen and alder are home to mule deer, Rocky Mountain elk, blue grouse, and a variety of songbirds. Mountain goats caper on the rocky ridge below the lookout. Red-tailed hawks, goshawks, and golden eagles are seen from the Timberwolf vantage or along roads.

Viewing Information: High probability of seeing mountain goats year-round; in summer and fall, look along the road leading to Timberwolf. Mule deer, elk, and forest birds are common on Forest Service Road 1500 and Timberwolf Mountain spur road. Mountain usually snowed in late October through June.

Ownership: USFS (509-653-2205)
Size: Approximately fifty acres
Closest Town: Naches

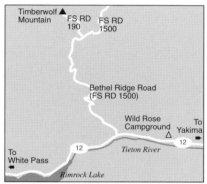

52 YAKIMA RIVER CANYON

Description: The Yakima River and Highway 821 wind through a scenic canyon, home to California bighorn sheep, golden and bald eagles, prairie falcons, and other raptors. Umtanum Canyon trail provides good opportunities to view woodpeckers, songbirds, valley quail, and chukar partridge.

Viewing Information: High probability of seeing bighorn sheep on the slopes of Manastash Ridge. Bald eagles roost along the river from November through February. Cross the suspension bridge at the north end of Umtanum Recreation Site to reach Umtanum Canyon trail. Wildflowers in spring and early summer.

Ownership: BLM; WDNR
(509-575-2740); WDFW
Size: Twenty-mile canyon
Closest Town: Yakima, Ellensburg

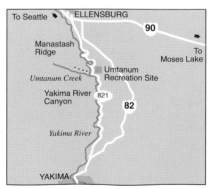

53 RED TOP MOUNTAIN

Description: One of the best hawk watching spots in Washington. Teanaway Ridge serves as a handrail for migrating ospreys; golden and bald eagles; Cooper's, sharp-shinned, and red-tailed hawks; and turkey vultures. Other wildlife includes mule deer, Rocky Mountain elk, and a variety of songbirds.

Viewing Information: Best viewing is in September and October, with a high probability of seeing Cooper's and sharp-shinned hawks. Deer and elk are common on the lookout road in spring, summer, and fall, as are Clark's nutcrackers, pygmy owls, and mountain songbirds. Wildflowers in late spring and early summer.

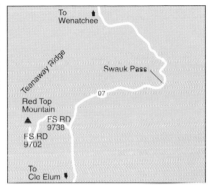

Ownership: USFS (509-674-4411)
Size: One acre
Closest Town: Cle Elum

54 ICICLE CREEK CANYON

Description: At more than 8,000 feet from floor to rim, Icicle Canyon is one of the deepest canyons in the Pacific Northwest. Mule deer forage along the creek; golden eagles and other raptors soar overhead. Harlequin ducks and other waterfowl nest here. Leavenworth National Fish Hatchery on Icicle Creek provides viewing of chinook salmon. Osprey and great blue herons stalk fish near the hatchery.

Viewing Information: Raptors and waterfowl best viewed in spring and summer. From the hatchery, follow two-mile interpretive trail. Another trail heads upstream along Snow Creek into the Alpine Lakes Wilderness Area.

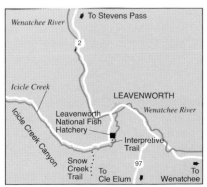

Ownership: USFWS; USFS (509-548-7641 or 548-1413)
Size: Twenty miles of road
Closest Town: Leavenworth

63

CASCADE MOUNTAINS

55 SWAKANE CANYON

Description: The open, grassy slopes and wooded draws of Swakane Canyon demonstrate the Cascade rainshadow effect and provide important mule deer wintering habitat. Also watch for bighorn sheep, golden eagles, and yellow-pine chipmunks. Mountain bluebirds, gray jays, blue grouse, valley quail, and a number of woodpecker species live here. Wildflowers are abundant.

Viewing Information: High probability of seeing bighorn sheep and many deer from December through March. During severe winters, deer are fed at sta-tions in the lower canyon, accessible by snowshoe or cross-country skis. Bighorn sheep frequent the south-facing slope about two miles from Swakane Wildlife Area entrance. Golden eagles and other raptors are seen year-round.

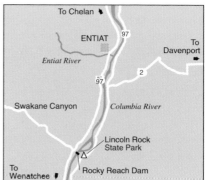

Ownership: USFS (509-784-1511); WDFW (509-575-2740)
Size: Eight-mile canyon
Closest Town: Wenatchee

56 GOLD CREEK POND

Description: Gold Creek Pond offers good viewing of active beaver lodges, nesting Canada geese and other waterfowl, and wading birds such as great blue herons. Black-tailed deer and Rocky Mountain elk are common in the area. A pair of osprey nest near the pond. Dolly Varden trout and kokanee salmon spawn in the creek.

Viewing Information: Moderate probability of seeing deer and elk; best chances in spring. Salmon spawn in September and October. The Forest Ser-vice has constructed a paved, barrier-free interpretive trail. Another trail and viewing pool are planned for observing spawning fish. Open year-round for day use.

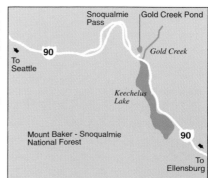

Ownership: USFS (425-888-1421); WDOT
Size: Fifteen-acre pond
Closest Town: North Bend

64

Description: An all-day commercial boat trip up Lake Chelan offers unrivaled views of some of the most rugged and scenic mountains in the Cascades, including the Sawtooth Range and Glacier Peak Wilderness. A glacial trough, Lake Chelan is one of the deepest lakes in North America. The lake is flanked on both sides by unroaded forest with a wide variety of habitats and wildlife viewing opportunities. Mule deer and mountain goats caper on the steep slopes and drainages. Black bear and even mountain lions are sometimes seen on the shore. Osprey dive for fish; golden and bald eagles scan for prey from treetop perches or on the wing. Waterfowl nest along the lake shore; look for harlequin ducks near the mouth of the Stehekin River.

Viewing Information: High probability of seeing mule deer and mountain goats in fall, winter, and spring. Low to moderate probability of seeing black bear and cougar. Ospreys are common in summer. Eagles can be seen at various times of the year. Nesting waterfowl are common in spring and summer.

The boat trip begins in the town of Chelan and ends in Stehekin, where the National Park Service has a visitor center. A short bus trip can be arranged to scenic Rainbow Falls or hikers can walk the Purple Creek Trail.

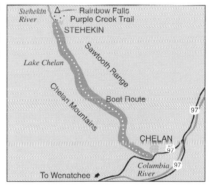

Ownership: Lake Chelan Boat Company (509-682-2224)
Size: Fifty miles
Closest Town: Chelan

The beaver is the largest native rodent in North America. Once overtrapped in Washington, beaver are fairly common again. Ponds created by these aquatic mammals provide excellent flood control benefits, and habitat for many species of fish and other wildlife.
TOM & PAT LEESON

Washington Biodiversity:

The Rainshadow Effect

Why does Washington have so many different plant and animal communities? In a word—water. Water is one of the biggest influences on biodiversity in any place. In Washington, the interaction of land, sea, and air create dramatically different rainfall patterns across the state, a major factor in determining the species of plants and animals that live in an area.

The coast of Washington is exposed to westerly winds that often travel 4,000 miles across the Pacific Ocean before reaching land. These winds are moisture-laden and warmed by ocean currents. As westerly winds reach the coast, the air rises and cools, dropping heavy precipitation on the Olympics and other coastal mountains.

Annual rainfall on the western slope of the Olympics exceeds 100 inches—the highest total anywhere in the U.S. outside of Alaska. Plant life is prolific here, with dense stands of Sitka spruce, western hemlock, and western red cedar, with a lush undergrowth of moss, ferns, vine maple, and trillium.

The Olympic mountains also create what is called a

rainshadow effect: by causing most rain to fall on the coastal, or western slope, the mountains shield the Puget Sound basin from the heaviest precipitation. Rainfall on the eastern side of the Olympics ranges from seventeen to about fifty inches per year.

As Pacific Ocean weather systems move inland, they encounter a second, even larger climatic barrier in the form of the Cascade Mountains. If there is any moisture left in a weather system at this point, the Cascades will capture most of it. Many Cascade peaks such as Mount Rainier and Mount Baker have permanent snowpack and glaciers. Low-elevation forests on the Cascades' west slope are often dominated by Douglas-fir, with a dense undergrowth of salal, ferns, Oregon grape, and creeping raspberry.

By the time westerly winds clear these two mountain ranges, they contain little or no moisture. Plant communities in eastern Washington are well-suited to this arid climate. The east slope of the Cascades is usually dominated by ponderosa pine, scrub oak, and sagebrush. The Columbia Basin, the lowest, warmest, and driest region of the state, is a true desert, with thousands of acres of shrub-steppe vegetation, characterized by sagebrush and native bunchgrasses.

58 MOUNTAIN LOOP HIGHWAY

Description: The scenic Mountain Loop Highway passes through forested, riparian, and alpine habitats typical of the west slope of the Cascade Mountains. Black-tailed deer, mountain goats, bald eagles, Pacific salmon, osprey, and a variety of mountain songbirds may be viewed on this three-hour loop drive.

Viewing Information: The loop highway begins in the foothills near Granite Falls, then follows the South Fork Stillaguamish River. The road skirts the jagged high country of the Henry M. Jackson Wilderness, then parallels the Sauk River on its long journey to the Skagit River and Puget Sound. The first stop on the loop is the Granite Falls Fishway on the South Fork Stillaguamish, where various runs of pink, chinook, and coho salmon may be viewed negotiating the fish ladder on their upstream migration to spawn above the falls. A trail (maintenance road) leads to an observation area. Gold Basin Pond, upstream on the South Fork, is a shallow, former mill pond, where migrating coho salmon may be viewed from October through February. Bald eagles can also be seen here taking advantage of the late-fall and winter salmon runs. Osprey, great blue herons, and waterfowl are commonly viewed here in spring and summer. The pond also provides nesting and rearing habitat for waterfowl. Further up the highway, Big Four Boardwalk has views of beaver dams, waterfowl, and songbirds. Monte Cristo Lake and Bedal Creek offer great views of Cascade Crest peaks; mountain goats can be seen from a distance in fall and winter on cliffs. On the Sauk River Bench, there is a high probability of encountering deer in fall and winter. Bald eagles also winter along the Sauk from November to March. The last designated stop on the Mountain Loop is Beaver Lake Trail, a three-mile hike along an old railroad grade following the Sauk River. Watch for river otters or beaver in ponds along the trail.

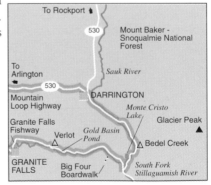

Ownership: WDF; USFS (360-436-1155)
Size: Fifty-four-mile loop (three-hour drive)
Closest Town: Granite Falls, Darrington

59 FORTSON MILL PONDS

Description: These two spring-fed ponds on the North Fork Stillaguamish River are connected by a system of streams, beaver ponds, and wetlands. Beaver, river otter, muskrat, and waterfowl ripple the placid surface of the ponds. Chum and coho salmon spawn here, as well as pink and chinook salmon, and steelhead trout. Cutthroat trout are plentiful. Osprey, kingfishers, and great blue herons feed here.

Viewing Information: Spawning chum and coho salmon crowd the outlet streams from mid-October through January. Look for other salmon and steelhead trout beginning August and September.

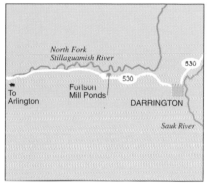

Ownership: WDFW (360-753-6600)
Size: Seven acres
Closest Town: Darrington

60 UPPER SKAGIT BALD EAGLE AREA

Description: This stretch of the upper Skagit River hosts one of the largest and most visible populations of wintering bald eagles in the lower forty-eight states. Spawned-out salmon carcasses become the wintering eagles' main food source. Eagles can be viewed feeding on the gravel bars or roosting in trees.

Viewing Information: Eagle migration coincides with spawning runs of chum, coho, and other salmon species on the upper Skagit River and tributaries. Eagles present November to mid-March; peaking in early January. The Nature Conservancy and public agencies work to protect wintering habitat for eagles. Best viewing areas along Highway 20 at Howard Miller Steelhead Park, Washington Eddy Lookout, and Sutter Creek Rest Area.

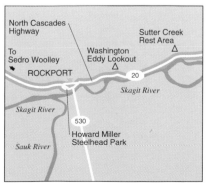

Ownership: Mixed. Upper Skagit Bald Eagle Festival (360-853-7009)
Size: Eight miles from Rockport to Marblemount
Closest Town: Rockport, Concrete

CASCADE MOUNTAINS

61 NORTH CASCADES HIGHWAY

Description: Passing through North Cascades National Park, Highway 20 gives motorists and hikers access to some of the most beautiful mountain scenery and outstanding wildlife habitat in North America.

Viewing Information: The Skagit River Bald Eagle Natural Area is discussed on page 69. Eagles can also be seen along the upper Skagit in the Ross Lake National Recreation Area. Black-tailed deer are often visible in the community of Newhalem and mountain goats can sometimes be viewed on nearby south-facing rocks. Also near Newhalem, summer chinook and pink salmon can be observed spawning in Goodell Creek and the Skagit River from late August through October. Large numbers of chinook, pink, coho, and chum salmon are seen in nearby Park Slough Spawning Channel, on the south side of the river, from August through December. Fish-eaters such as raccoons, otters, and coyotes frequent areas where salmon spawn. The Diablo Lake Overlook near Ross Dam is a good place to hear and maybe see pikas, small, short-eared rabbit relatives that live in rocky, alpine areas. Golden-mantled ground squirrels are also common here. The nearby Happy Creek Forest Walk is a short, barrier-free trail through an old growth forest. A hike up aptly named Beaver Creek offers a chance to see beaver and other streamside wildlife. Rainy Pass, near the crest of the Cascades, offers rest stop and picnic facilities and a one-mile, barrier-free trail to Lake Ann. Look and listen for the whistling sound of hoary marmots, which often coexist with pikas in rock piles along the highway. The backcountry of the park and Ross Lake National Recreation Area can only be reached by foot trail, but it is still possible to occasionally see reclusive wildlife such as black bear from the highway corridor. Timber wolves and grizzly bears, both listed as endangered, are known to be in this area, but chances of viewing these animals are extremely slim. THE NORTH CASCADES HIGHWAY IS CLOSED BY SNOW IN WINTER.

Ownership: WDFW; NPS (360-856-5700)

Size: Sedro Woolley to Rainy Pass: approximately ninety miles

Closest Town: Concrete

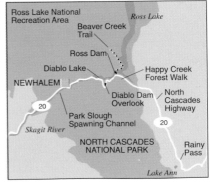

62 METHOW WILDLIFE AREA

Description: A mix of shrub-steppe and forest habitats provide critical winter range for the largest herd of mule deer in the state. Deer are common on south- and west-facing slopes, such as those above Pearrygin Lake. Male blue grouse are heard booming and are sometimes seen during mating season. Great views of the Methow Valley and North Cascades.

Viewing Information: High probability of seeing deer from mid-March through May. Grouse mating season usually in April. Deer, grouse, chipmunks, warblers, and other songbirds are seen on roads and trails near Bear Creek campground. Wintering bald eagles are seen along the Methow River between towns of Winthrop and Twisp. OPEN FOR DEER HUNTING SEPTEMBER-OCTOBER. ROADS USUSALLY SNOWED IN DECEMBER 15-MARCH 15.

Ownership: WDFW (509-754-4624)
Size: 16,000 acres
Closest Town: Winthrop

Bald eagles were almost driven to extinction by eggshell thinning caused by the pesticide DDT. With a nationwide ban on DDT in the 1970s, eagles, osprey, and many other birds of prey have made a dramatic comeback. Washington now hosts more wintering bald eagles than any other state except Alaska.
LEE MANN

71

REGION 5: NORTHEAST WASHINGTON

The high country of northeast Washington is dominated by the densely-forested Okanogan Highlands, including the Selkirk Mountain Range. Separate from the Cascades, the mountains here are shielded from most Pacific Ocean weather patterns. The Selkirk Range, which extends into the far northeast corner of the state, is actually part of the Rocky Mountain system, with eroded topography and long mountain meadows.

Wildlife of the Okanogan Highlands reflects a transition between the Cascades and Rockies, with many wildlife species common to both, such as mule deer and white-tailed deer. The Selkirks provide habitat for Rocky Mountain species found nowhere else in Washington, including moose, woodland caribou, and the state's only fully-documented population of grizzly bears, listed as an endangered species.

Photo, opposite page: Goat Rocks Wilderness. **PAT O'HARA**

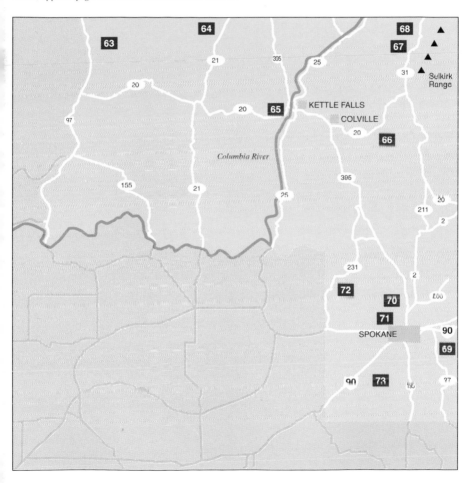

63	Virginia Lilly Old Growth Trail	**69**	Liberty Lake County Park
64	Little Vulcan Mountain	**70**	Riverside State Park:
65	Sherman Creek-Growden		Little Spokane River Natural Area
	Heritage Site	**71**	Riverside State Park:
66	Little Pend Orielle Wildlife Management Area		Deep Creek Canyon
		72	Devil's Gap
67	Big Meadow Lake	**73**	Turnbull National Wildlife Refuge
68	Flume Creek Mountain Goat Viewing Area		

63 VIRGINIA LILLY OLD GROWTH TRAIL

Description: This interpretive trail wends through an old growth forest of Douglas-fir, western larch, and ponderosa pine. The grove harbors goshawks, great gray owls, pileated woodpeckers, and other secretive species. Watch for white-tailed and mule deer, red squirrels, and a variety of songbirds and woodpeckers along the trail. Wildflowers, including Indian paintbrush and arrow leaf balsam root, are abundant. Higher elevations offer views of the North Cascades and the Kettle Range.

Viewing Information: High probability of seeing deer, small mammals, and songbirds from the trail. Parking at trailhead and on roadside.

Ownership: USFS (509-486-2186)
Size: Three-mile trail
Closest Town: Tonasket

64 LITTLE VULCAN MOUNTAIN

Description: This unique canyon wall site in the Kettle River Valley is home to a conspicuous herd of bighorn sheep. Forests, open grassy slopes, aspen groves, and small springs also harbor mule deer. Yellow-bellied marmots bask in the sun atop rocks. Red-tailed hawks and golden eagles soar on canyon updrafts.

Viewing Information: High probability of seeing bighorn sheep off West Kettle River Road year-round; best in early spring and fall. Binoculars or spotting scope recommended. Moderate to high probability of seeing mule deer and birds of prey. Marmots most active in summer. Primitive area. Trail is steep. CARRY DRINKING WATER.

Ownership: BLM; USFS; WDNR
Size: 1,840 acres of public land
Closest Town: Curlew

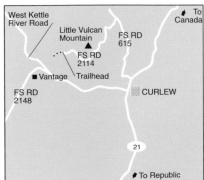

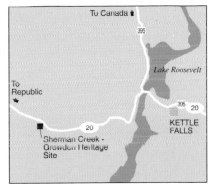

Description: Sherman Creek and adjacent wet meadows provide important open space and aquatic habitat in a dense forest of mixed conifers. White-tailed deer forage here. Watch for moose, which are expanding their range in northeast Washington; also beaver, blue and ruffed grouse, mountain chickadees, and Steller's and gray jays. Native trout live in the creek and waterfowl nest here in spring.

Viewing Information: High probability of seeing white-tailed deer year-round. Beaver are active on Sherman Creek. Low to moderate probability of seeing moose in spring and summer. In spring and summer, look for grouse, chickadees, and jays along forest trails. Additional barrier-free trails, juvenile fishing access, and major interpretive facilities are being developed. Part of the Sherman Pass National Scenic Byway.

Ownership: WDFW; USFS
(509-738-6111)
Size: Ten acres
Closest Town: Kettle Falls

The great gray owl is the largest owl in North America. In Washington, it is usually confined to higher elevation forests of the Cascades and Okanogan Highlands.
TOM & PAT LEESON

66 LITTLE PEND OREILLE WILDLIFE REFUGE

Description: Rolling ponderosa pine national forests, quiet river bottoms, and lakes are home to an abundance of wildlife and diverse mixed conifer on the west slope of the Selkirk Range. White-tailed and mule deer, black bear, ruffed and blue grouse, and numerous songbirds inhabit the forests and riparian areas. Beaver are active in the streams; dabbling ducks, other waterfowl, and birds of prey are common along streams, wetlands, and forested lakes.

Viewing Information: High probability of seeing white-tailed deer, grouse, and songbirds. Mule deer are seen at higher elevations. Possibility of seeing black bear in the spring and fall. Beaver lodges and dams can be seen along the Rookery Road. Look for waterfowl at McDowell Lake. Interior gravel roads are open most of the year. Stay on Watchable Wildlife loop unless you have good maps and time to explore logging roads. Five very primitive campgrounds. PLEASE DO NOT DRIVE OFF ROAD. CARRY YOUR OWN WATER. CHECK AT REFUGE OFFICE FOR ROAD CONDITIONS, CAMPGROUND AND TRAIL LOCATIONS, AND FALL HUNTING SEASONS.

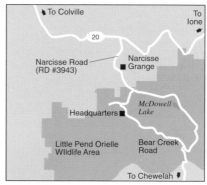

Ownership: USFWS; (509-684-8384)
Size: 40,000 acres
Closest Town: Colville

Moose are steadily expanding their range into Washington. Each year, moose sightings are on the rise from the Selkirk Mountains, in northeast Washington, as far south as Spokane.
DEBI OTTINGER

67 BIG MEADOW LAKE

Description: This forested mountain lake and wetlands are a magnet for wildlife typical of the Selkirk Range. White-tailed and mule deer are common; also watch for moose and beaver. Goldeneyes, buffleheads, and other ducks migrate from the coast to nest on small islands and around lake shore.

Viewing Information: High probability of seeing deer on roads and around lake; moose are best seen near dawn and dusk. Beaver reside on Big Meadow Creek. Good chance of seeing osprey in spring and summer. Barrier-free Big Meadow Trail leads to observation tower with excellent view of wetlands. From the campground, take Meadow Magic Trail around the lake.

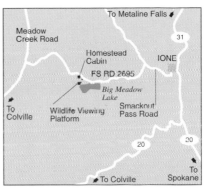

Ownership: USFS (509-684 7060)
Size: Seventy-acre lake
Closest Town: Ione

68 FLUME CREEK MOUNTAIN GOAT VIEWING AREA

Description: The forests and high meadows around Flume Creek are home to wildlife found nowhere else in Washington. One of the most reliable places to observe mountain goats; other species present include bighorn sheep, moose, woodland caribou, and white-tailed and mule deer. This site won the national U.S. Forest Service "Eyes on Wildlife" award in 1992.

Viewing Information: Excellent viewing of bighorn sheep at Hall Mountain December 1-March 1. Moose are sometimes seen along streams and meadows. Mountain goats are best viewed from late March through May or June. Also one of the highest diversities of breeding songbirds in Washington.

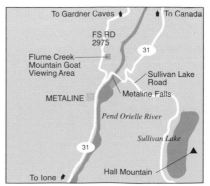

Ownership: USFS (509-446-7500)
Size: One acre
Closest Town: Metaline

69 LIBERTY LAKE COUNTY PARK

Description: Liberty Lake Marsh is a magnet for waterfowl, great blue herons and other wading birds, and birds of prey, including ospreys. A nearby old growth cedar grove and adjacent forested ridges are home to mule deer, Rocky Mountain elk, black bear, and yellow-bellied marmot.

Viewing Information: Upper end of the park features an information center and a barrier-free boardwalk with interpretive signs leading into Liberty Lake Marsh. High probability of seeing nesting waterfowl in spring and wading birds in spring and summer. Liberty Creek Trail begins at the campground and follows the creek through old growth cedar forest to a ridge top and Idaho state line. Views of the lake, Spokane Valley, and Idaho forests. High probability of seeing mule deer and songbirds along trail. Look for marmots in rocky areas. Low probability of seeing black bear or Rocky Mountain elk.

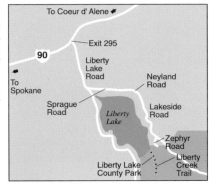

Ownership: Spokane County Parks and Recreation (509-456-4732)
Size: 3,000 acres
Closest Town: Spokane

Marmots are the largest members of the squirrel family. Like their eastern relative, the woodchuck, marmots emerge from hibernation to breed in early spring.
FRED PFLUGHOFT

70 RIVERSIDE STATE PARK: LITTLE SPOKANE RIVER NATURAL AREA

Description: The Little Spokane River meanders through a narrow, scenic valley to its confluence with the Spokane River. Ponderosa pine forest covers the ridge tops. Large cottonwoods and dense understory along river provide nesting sites for osprey and waterfowl, including diving ducks. Great blue heron roost here, and songbirds are common. Also watch for white-tailed deer, coyotes, beaver, and porcupines.

Viewing Information: Year-round hiking, canoeing, and kayaking. High probability of seeing great blue herons roosting in cottonwoods. Waterfowl are common in spring and summer. Low to moderate probability of seeing beaver, porcupines, coyotes, and deer. Songbirds are abundant in spring and summer. Wintering bald eagles are commonly seen near the mouth of the Little Spokane. Six-mile walking trail along the river. Well marked trailheads and canoe put-in sites well marked; upper put-in is closed in winter. Petroglyphs at downstream trailhead. Look for osprey in nests along the Spokane River in spring and early summer. ORGANIZED GROUPS CHECK WITH PARK HEADQUARTERS

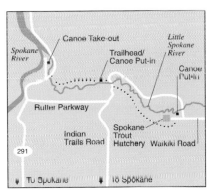

Ownership: WSP (509-456-3964)
Size: Six-mile trail
Closest Town: Spokane

Only six miles from downtown Spokane, the Little Spokane River Natural Area provides a quiet, shaded sanctuary for wildlife and people alike. PAT O'HARA

71 RIVERSIDE STATE PARK: DEEP CREEK CANYON

Description: A dense conifer forest gives way to large basaltic rock formations and this deep canyon, home to warblers and other songbirds. Canyon wrens nest here; their distinctive song echoes off the rock walls. White-tailed deer and Cooper's hawks are residents; osprey and bald eagles are also seen.

Viewing Information: Osprey nest along the Spokane River; look for wintering bald eagles at dusk. Listen for wrens and other songbirds in spring and summer. Deer and Cooper's hawks are seen year-round. From the trailhead at the mouth of Deep Creek (on the Centennial Trail), walk up the creek bed or take the wooded trail bordering the canyon. Deep Creek Canyon can also be seen from State Park Drive.

Ownership: WSP (509-456-3964)
Size: 275 acres
Closest Town: Spokane

72 DEVIL'S GAP

Description: Rock outcroppings, small canyons, and open forest support mule deer and numerous birds. Red-tailed hawks, turkey vultures, bald and golden eagles, and osprey soar over the Spokane River. Western bluebirds, canyon wrens, and the Lewis' woodpecker live in upland areas.

Viewing Information: High probability of seeing deer year-round. Osprey are seen in spring and summer from picnic area at Long Lake Dam. Up to thirty wintering bald eagles perch downstream from dam. Look for Lewis' woodpecker in spring and summer. Use roads and hiking trails from the dam site park or from trailhead on Devil's Gap Road.

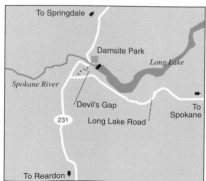

Ownership: Washington Water Power (509-482-4486)
Size: 300 acres
Closest Town: Reardon

Description: More than 130 lakes, ponds, and marshes dot these Channeled Scablands, so named for the erosional scars left by great floods at the end of the last ice age. Surrounded by open Ponderosa pine forest, Turnbull is an important stopover for migrating waterfowl of the Pacific Flyway. Many species nest here, including Canada geese, scaup, redheads, ruddy ducks, and green-winged, blue-winged, and cinnamon teal. Bird watchers also enjoy many species of songbirds and birds of prey. Watch for badgers, coyotes, and Rocky Mountain elk. Wildflowers are abundant.

Viewing Information: Songbirds and birds of prey can be seen in spring and summer. High probability of seeing nesting swans, geese, and ducks in spring and summer. Good chance of seeing badgers, coyotes, and birds of prey in spring and summer. A small herd of elk spends part of the year on the refuge. Wildflowers are best in spring. Six-mile auto tour with many vantage points and trailheads; pamphlet available at refuge headquarters. Environmental education opportunities for groups.

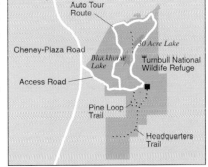

Ownership: USFWS (509-235-4723)
Size: 15,500 acres (2,200 acres open to the public)
Closest Town: Cheney

Western bluebirds are cavity nesters, using abandoned woodpecker holes or natural cavities in trees. The red breast of the male bluebird, like the robin, signals aggression toward other males of the species.
TOM & PAT LEESON

81

REGION 6: COLUMBIA BASIN - SOUTHEAST WASHINGTON

Located in the double rainshadow of the Olympic and Cascade Mountains, the Columbia Basin is the warmest and driest region of the state. Originally carved by glaciers and slowly eroded over time by the Columbia River, the basin was further sculpted about 12,000 years ago by a series of violent flows known as the Spokane Floods. The floods left behind strange basaltic rock formations known as the Channeled Scablands. The basin is characterized by native shrub-steppe vegetation and thousands of acres of ponds and marshes created by irrigation water from the Columbia Basin Project. Southwest Washington includes the vast wheatfields of the Palouse Hills and the rugged Blue Mountains which straddle the border between Washington and Oregon.

Wildlife of this region include the golden eagle, prairie falcon, and other species commonly found in high shrub-steppe deserts of the West. The Columbia Basin is also a magnet for thousands of ducks, geese, and migratory wading birds that nest and winter in this vast system of ponds and marshes. The Blue Mountains harbor a variety of wildlife species found in dry mountain areas, including mule deer, bighorn sheep and Rocky Mountain elk.

Photo, opposite page: Shrub-steppe habitat, Wilson Creek Canyon. **SUNNY WALTER**

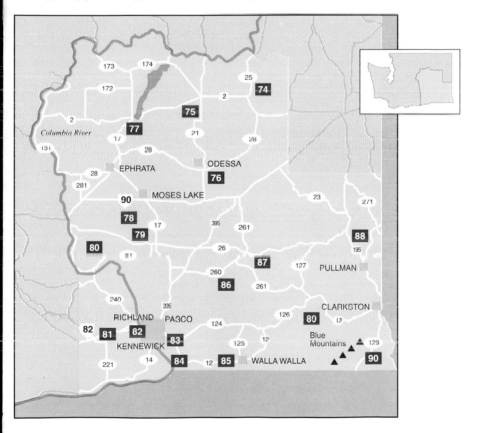

74	Dodd-Olsen Canyon	83	McNary National Wildlife Refuge
75	Wilson Creek Canyon	84	Wallula Habitat Management Unit
76	Channeled Scablands Desert Loop	85	Whitman Mission National Historic Site
77	Dry Falls-Sun Lakes State Park	86	Lower Monumental Lock and Dam
78	Desert Wildlife Area	87	Palouse Falls State Park
79	Columbia National Wildlife Refuge	88	Kamiak Butte County Park
80	Crab Creek Coulee	89	William T. Wooten Wildlife Area
81	Badger Slope	90	Chief Joseph Wildlife Area
82	Yakima River Delta Wildlife Park		

74 DODD-OLSEN CANYON

Description: This area is farmed and intensively managed for white-tailed and mule deer and other wildlife. Ruffed and blue grouse inhabit wooded draws; Columbian sharp-tailed grouse favor open areas. Woodpeckers and songbirds are common, as are red-tailed hawks, golden eagles, and other raptors. Introduced Rio Grande turkeys are present but elusive.

Viewing Information: Farm road allows foot access to Dodd Canyon. High probability of seeing deer year-round; up to 300 deer IN WINTER. Moderate probability of seeing woodpeckers, songbirds, raptors, and grouse in spring and summer. Look for Columbian sharp-tailed grouse in spring. Wildflowers plentiful in spring.

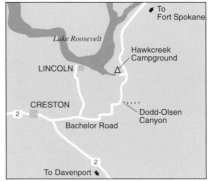

Ownership: WDFW (509-456-4082)
Size: 340 acres
Closest Town: Creston

75 WILSON CREEK CANYON

Description: This basalt-rimmed canyon is one of the finest examples of native shrub-steppe habitat in the state. Wildflowers include Indian paintbrush, lupine, phlox, and larkspur. Red-tailed and ferruginous hawks, great horned owls, golden eagles, and prairie falcons are seen here. Valley quail are common. Pintails, redheads, and cinnamon teal nest here. Bobcats, badgers, and coyotes are more elusive.

Viewing Information: Barrier-free trail through sagebrush and bunchgrass. Wildflowers are abundant in spring. High probability of seeing raptors from Wilson Creek overlook. Watch for waterfowl in spring and summer.

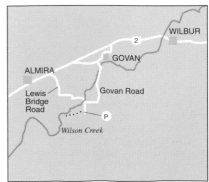

Ownership: BLM (509-353-2570)
Size: 600 acres
Closest Town: Wilbur

Description: The maze of cliffs, channels, canyons, lava caves, and strange rock formations known as the Channeled Scablands was sculpted about 12,000 years ago by violent glacial floods. Commonly known as the Spokane Floods, these are the largest floods ever documented—yet they occurred over a matter of days! This five-hour auto tour provides excellent views of mule deer, chukar partridge, valley quail, waterfowl, desert songbirds, and a variety of raptors, including golden eagles, prairie falcons, ferruginous hawks, and great horned owls. Wildflowers are plentiful in spring and early summer.

Viewing Information: Begin the loop at Ritzville on Interstate 90 and drive north to Rocky Ford on Crab Creek (1), where desert songbirds, waterfowl, and mule deer are often seen along the stream. Access by permission only. Crab Creek Canyon, further downstream, is an excellent example of a prehistoric flood channel; golden eagles can sometimes be viewed on the basalt columns and rock formations. Continue north to Coal Creek (2), home to upland birds, waterfowl, and mule deer; this is public land, open for hiking and exploration. The next stop, Seven Springs Road (3), crosses one of Washington's last remaining habitats for the Columbian sharp-tailed grouse. To the southwest, down Lake Creek Canyon, glimpse the westernmost grove of ponderosa pine in this desert region. Wilson Creek Canyon (4), southwest of Wilbur, is discussed in site 75. South of Almira, the road crosses Wilson Creek at the Kiner Ranch (5). The last designated stop, just north of Odessa, is the BLM's Lakeview Ranch (6), one of the last places in the Columbia Basin where the public may see sage grouse. The ranch is open for hiking and primitive camping, with some fire restrictions in summer and fall. West of ranch headquarters, hiking trails extend into a maze of canyons, including scenic Lake Creek Canyon. The drive begins and ends at Interstate 90 but can be accessed at a number of places. Roads are crooked and narrow in places. WATCH FOR LIVESTOCK AND SLOW-MOVING TRAFFIC.

Ownership: Visitor's guide available through the Odessa Economic Development Council (509-982-2232)
Size: 150-mile loop (five-hour drive)
Closest Town: Ritzville, Odessa
Directions: Numbers 1-6 on map identify tour stops described above.

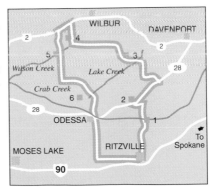

77 DRY FALLS-SUN LAKES STATE PARK

Description: Dry Falls is the former site of one of the largest waterfalls in geologic history. Downstream from the falls is a long chain of lakes bordered by freshwater marshes, shrub-steppe desert, and basalt rock formations. The Sun Lakes chain is on the migration route for many species of waterfowl, shorebirds, and songbirds. Breeding pairs of Barrow's goldeneyes, Canada geese, redheads, and yellow-headed and red-winged blackbirds nest in the wetlands. Rough-legged hawks and a few bald eagles winter here. Mule deer, chukar partridge, and valley quail are common.

Viewing Information: Excellent viewing most of the year. In April and May, migrating waterfowl rest and feed on these lakes, including Soap Lake. Breeding waterfowl and blackbirds are abundant in spring and summer. Raptors can be seen year-round. Dry Falls Interpretive Center offers good viewing of raptors and other wildlife in the Sun Lakes chain. Sun Lakes State Park offers camping.

Ownership: WSP; NPS (509-632-5214)
Size: Twenty-mile-long chain of lakes
Closest Town: Ephrata

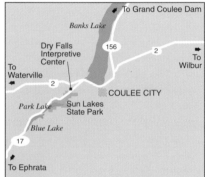

Redhead ducks spend their winters in the southern United States. Each spring they migrate thousands of miles to nest and raise young in the potholes and desert marshes of eastern Washington.
DARRELL GULIN

78 | DESERT WILDLIFE AREA

Description: The area south and west of Moses Lake is one of the best places in the state to view waterfowl, marsh birds, raptors, and many species of shorebirds. Native shrub-steppe desert and stabilized sand dunes intermix with cultivated land and a huge system of reservoirs, potholes, marshes, and "wasteways," all created by irrigation water from the Columbia Basin Project. Canada geese, mallards, avocets, black-necked stilts, and Wilson's phalaropes gather here by the thousands. Herons, egrets, cormorants, and riparian songbirds are common. White pelicans are sometimes seen in the Potholes area.

Viewing Information: A major stopover for Canada geese and mallards in fall and winter. Other ducks, geese and migratory wading birds, including avocets, black-necked stilts, and Wilson's phalaropes nest here in spring and summer. Wildlife can be seen from a number of parking areas and trailheads along the main roads. Winchester Wasteway, near its intersection with Dodson Road, is a good place to spot mating avocets and stilts in April and May. Further south, an easy trail goes east along the swift-moving Frenchman Hills Wasteway, providing good viewing of herons, egrets, waterfowl, and songbirds. West of Dodson Road, on Frenchman Hills Road, burrowing owls are sometimes seen in spring and summer living in the abandoned dens of badgers and other mammals. Excellent viewing by small boat or canoe.

Ownership: USBR; WDFW (509-754-4624)
Size: 60,000 acres
Closest Town: Moses Lake

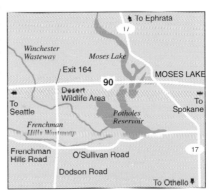

Sometimes known as a jacksnipe or Wilson's snipe, the common snipe is a familiar sight in Washington's wet lowlands. The snipe's spring mating call is thought to be made by air rushing through its tail feathers.
RON SPOMER

79 | COLUMBIA NATIONAL WILDLIFE REFUGE

Description: The ponds, streams, and marshes here are a magnet for thousands of Canada geese, mallards, and other migratory waterfowl that winter over or stop·to rest and feed during their fall migration. Wading birds such as avocets and long-billed curlews nest here. Hundreds of sandhill cranes feed in nearby farm fields for a short time during migration.

Viewing Information: Much of the refuge is closed during fall and winter but opens again in spring. Sandhill cranes are seen in March and early April. Rough-legged hawks, burrowing owls, and other wildlife common to the Channeled Scablands can be viewed at various times of the year. Wildflowers are abundant in spring and early summer. A twenty-two-mile loop drive includes an interpretive overlook at Royal Lake, where up to 10,000 ducks and geese gather in winter. Small boats without motors are allowed on some lakes and a canoe trail has been defined by the refuge. Three interpretive hiking trails through marsh, riparian, and upland shrub-steppe desert habitats originate at Morgan Lake Road. Primitive camping is allowed at Soda Lake and on adjacent state land. Check at refuge headquarters in Othello for maps and regulations on camping, boating, hunting, and hiking.

Ownership: USFWS (509-488-2668)
Size: 23,200 acres
Closest Town: Othello

With more than 3,700 acres of wetlands and open water near corn fields and other crops, Columbia National Wildlife Refuge provides ideal feeding and resting areas for migratory waterfowl. It is not uncommon to see more than 100,000 ducks and geese together on the refuge during the fall.
CURT GIVEN

Description: Crab Creek Coulee is a long, magnificent valley carved out of rock by glaciers and prehistoric floods; the stream is officially designated the longest creek in the United States. This perennial desert stream is bordered by shrub-steppe desert, sand dunes, riparian farmland, and towering basalt cliffs. Red-tailed hawks, golden eagles, and prairie falcons nest and roost in the cliffs. Chukar partridge, valley quail, and ring-necked pheasants are common. Coyotes hunt in the fields; badgers and burrowing owls are seen along the John Wayne Trail. Canada geese and dabbling ducks nest along the creek. Nunnally Lake and other deep pools harbor nesting goldeneyes and other diving ducks.

Viewing Information: Enter from Red Rock Coulee and follow Crab Creek downstream to Beverly, where it enters the Columbia River. High probability of seeing red-tailed hawks; low to moderate probability of seeing golden eagles and prairie falcons in spring and summer. Upland birds are common in spring, summer, and fall. Low to moderate probability of seeing coyotes, badgers, and burrowing owls in spring and summer. Watch for waterfowl in spring and summer. Many access points to John Wayne Trail (WDNR permit required), Crab Creek, and fishing lakes.

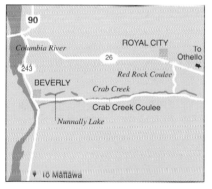

Ownership: WDW (509-754-4624)
Size: Approximately eighteen miles
Closest Town: Royal City

Prairie falcons are common in the open coulee country of eastern Washington, where they feed on songbirds, ground squirrels, and other small mammals.
ART WOLFE

81 BADGER SLOPE

Description: An impressive variety of raptors ride the thermals above these grassy bluffs and basalt outcroppings. Watch for red-tailed hawks, ferruginous hawks, turkey vultures, prairie falcons, and golden eagles. Raptors also nest on cliffs. Yellow-bellied marmots and burrowing owls are also seen here. Wildflowers, including lupine and wild daisies, are abundant in spring.

Viewing Information: High probability of seeing raptors in spring and summer. Owls and marmots are best seen in spring and summer. From the top of McBee Road, walk west on ridge to radio tower and beyond. Binoculars or spotting scope recommended. DO NOT APPROACH NESTING RAPTORS—THEY ARE PROTECTED BY LAW. ROAD FROM KIONA IS STEEP AND ROUGH.

Ownership: BLM (509-353-2570)
Size: 3,000 acres
Closest Town: Benton City

82 YAKIMA RIVER DELTA WILDLIFE PARK

Description: URBAN SITE. This wetland oasis attracts Canada geese and many species of dabbling ducks. Mule deer favor the dense forest of willow and Russian olive. Great blue herons and other wading birds are common.

Viewing Information: From Wye Neighborhood Park, walk across a short dike to Bateman Island or walk upstream as far as Yakima River bridge. High probability of seeing waterfowl year-round. Look for deer in early morning or evening. Many species of songbirds and small mammals such as cottontail rabbits are also seen on trail.

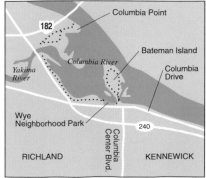

Ownership: ACE; City of Richland Parks (509-943-9161)
Size: 1,090 acres
Closest Town: Richland

83 | MCNARY NATIONAL WILDLIFE REFUGE

Description: These sloughs, marshes, and croplands offer excellent views of waterfowl and wading birds. Canada geese and ducks are common; avocets and long-billed curlews nest here. Look for yellow-headed blackbirds in marshes. White pelicans rest on Burbank Slough. Northern harriers, red-tailed hawks and burrowing owls inhabit the area.

Viewing Information: High probability of seeing waterfowl in fall, winter, and spring. Look for shorebirds, pelicans, and raptors in spring and summer. Some areas closed all or part of year; year-round viewing from perimeter roads. One-mile Burbank Slough Interpretive Trail is open year-round.

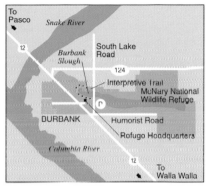

Ownership: USFWS (509 547-1912)
Size: 3,600 acres
Closest Town: Pasco

84 | WALLULA HABITAT MANAGEMENT UNIT

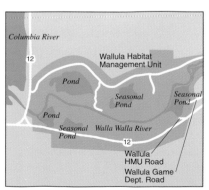

Description: These large seasonal ponds, bottomland forest, and croplands support Canada geese, goldeneyes, redheads, and cinnamon teal. Shorebirds, including avocets, long-billed curlews, and common snipe nest here. Watch for white pelicans, northern harriers, and red-tailed hawks.

Viewing Information: High probability of seeing geese and other waterfowl from late fall through February. High probability of seeing nesting ducks and migrating pelicans in spring and summer. Raptors seen year-round, especially in fields along river. Foot travel allowed on gated roads.

Ownership: ACE (503-922-3211)
Size: 2,100 acres
Closest Town: Pasco

85 WHITMAN MISSION NATIONAL HISTORIC SITE

Description: Well-known for its historical importance, this site also offers excellent year-round wildlife viewing. Up to 200 Canada geese and other waterfowl winter here. A barrier-free (but steep) trail leads to the top of Whitman Memorial Hill, where red-tailed hawks and northern harriers are seen hunting the cornfields. Mule deer, ring-necked pheasant, valley quail, and a variety of songbirds and small mammals are common during evening or early morning. Magpies and raptors roost and nest in cottonwoods and silver poplars.

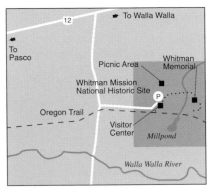

Viewing Information: High probability of seeing Canada geese and other waterfowl from mid-September through April.

Ownership: NPS (509-522-6360)
Size: Ninety-five acres
Closest Town: Walla Walla

86 LOWER MONUMENTAL LOCK AND DAM

Description: Fish ladders here allow passage and viewing of chinook salmon, steelhead trout, and other spawning fish as they migrate up the Snake River.

Viewing Information: Fish ladders are visible and a public viewing room is open year-round. Visiting hours vary according to season. Spring chinook arrive in April and viewing continues through summer and fall. The fall chinook run usually peaks in late September. Steelhead trout are seen throughout salmon migration. Steelhead runs usually peak in September or October. Spectacular spring wildflowers and mule deer viewing nearby Devil's Canyon, from Highway 260 to Lower Monumental Dam.

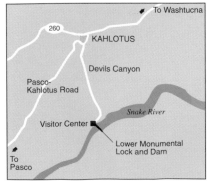

Ownership: ACE (509-547-7781)
Size: NA
Closest Town: Connell

Description: This 200-foot waterfall rivals the famous falls of Hawaii for sheer beauty, especially during spring and early summer when flows are high in the Palouse River. The park is a grassy, shaded oasis for wildlife surrounded by basalt rock formations and desert shrub-steppe habitat. Prairie falcons, golden eagles, Swainson's hawks, and other raptors nest in the canyon below the falls. Ravens and magpies scavenge here, and songbirds are common. Small mammals include yellow-bellied marmots and cottontail rabbits.

Viewing Information: Look for wildlife in Palouse Canyon downstream from the falls in the small park on the northern rim, and along Highway 261 and the 2.5-mile gravel road leading into the park. High probability of seeing songbirds, ravens, magpies, and marmots in spring and summer. Moderate probability of seeing raptors in spring and summer.

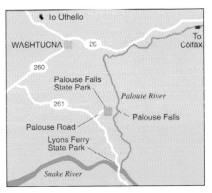

Ownership: WSP (509-646-3252)
Size: Eighty-three acres
Closest Town: Washtucna

Spectacular Palouse Falls was carved out of rock by the prehistoric Spokane Floods. These violent flows changed forever the landscape of eastern Washington.
PAT O'HARA

93

88 KAMIAK BUTTE COUNTY PARK

Description: A 3,000-foot forested island of rock in a sea of wheat fields, this park is a haven for warblers, nuthatches, pygmy and great horned owls, and white-tailed deer. From atop the butte, the Wallowa Mountains are visible more than 100 miles to the south.

Viewing Information: Pine Ridge Trail climbs 3.5 miles through mixed conifer forest to summit. Good probability of seeing songbirds and raptors in spring and summer. White-tailed deer are common year-round. Wildflowers in spring and early summer. County offers guided nature tours in summer.

Ownership: Whitman County Parks (509-397-6238)
Size: 298 acres
Closest Town: Pullman, Colfax

89 WILLIAM T. WOOTEN WILDLIFE AREA

Description: This site features wildlife typical of the Blue Mountains. Rocky Mountain elk and mule deer favor steep, sparsely timbered talus slopes and brushy draws. Look for bighorn sheep on Abels Ridge; white-tailed deer along the Tucannon River. Chukar partridge and mountain quail are seen in open areas. Introduced wild turkeys are more often heard than seen.

Viewing Information: High probability of seeing elk from mid-December into March; mule deer year-round. Whitetails are more elusive. Bighorn sheep easier to see in winter. Upland birds common in spring and summer; listen for turkeys in spring and fall. Wildflowers in spring and early summer.

Ownership: WDFW (509-456-4082)
Size: 11,000 acres
Closest Town: Pomeroy

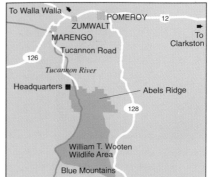

Description: The Nez Perce tribe once wintered in this deep, intricate chasm along Joseph Creek and the Grande Ronde River to take advantage of the warmer micro-climate on the canyon floor. Today, the towering rock formations, steep grassy slopes, and riparian habitat support an incredible diversity of wildlife. Mule deer and Rocky Mountain elk browse here. Golden eagles soar over the streams and prairie falcons perch on the rims. Upland birds include mountain quail and chukar partridge; also watch for mountain and western bluebirds.

Viewing Information: Wildlife viewing is best in spring. High probability of seeing mule deer along Joseph Creek and in irrigated farmlands. Look for elk in winter, when they migrate down from the Blue Mountains. Raptors are seen in spring and summer. Quail can be seen along Joseph Creek; chukar partridge are ubiquitous. Bluebirds migrate here in spring. Parking and other facilities are limited. Roads and jeep trails are open for foot or horse travel. Primitive camping.

Ownership: WDFW (509-456-4082)
Size: 9,000 acres
Closest Town: Asotin

Rocky Mountain and California bighorn sheep are both native to Washington. They were largely eliminated from the state by 1935 due to diseases transmitted by domestic livestock. Bighorns have been successfully reintroduced to many areas of their former range in the Cascade, Selkirk, and Blue mountains of southeast Washington.
SCOTT PRICE

POPULAR WILDLIFE VIEWING SPECIES OF WASHINGTON

The index below identifies forty of the more interesting, uncommon, or attractive wildlife species found in Washington, and some of the best sites for viewing them. Many of the animals listed may be viewed at other sites as well. The numbers following each species are site numbers, not page numbers.

SPECIES	SITE NUMBER
Bald eagle	5, 23, 25, 31, 35, 49, 60, 70
Beaver	4, 17, 42, 56, 58, 59, 65, 66
Bighorn sheep	47, 50, 52, 55, 64 (Hall Mtn.), 68
Black bear	8, 11, 20, 24, 47, 48, 66
Black brant	11-13, 25, 27, 33, 36, 37
Black oystercatcher	21-23, 27, 28
Black-tailed deer	6, 20-22, 24, 41, 48, 58
Brown pelican	12, 13
Burrowing owl	78, 79, 83
California gray whale	13, 21, 22, 38
California sea lion	13, 21, 29, 40
Canada goose	1-3, 7, 78, 79, 82, 85
Chinook salmon	4, 5, 22, 40, 45, 58, 61, 86
Coho salmon	4, 5, 40, 45, 58, 59
Columbian sharp-tailed grouse	74, 76
Dall's porpoise	26, 29, 30, 32
Golden eagle	6, 29, 52, 54, 57, 64, 80, 90
Great blue heron	33, 34, 39, 42-44, 59, 70
Harbor seal	11, 13, 19, 25, 26, 29, 31, 36

SPECIES	SITE NUMBER
Harlequin duck	20, 25, 27, 33, 36, 54, 57
Minke whale	30-32
Moose	65, 67, 68
Mountain goat	18, 48, 51, 57, 58, 61, 68
Mule deer	54, 55, 57, 62, 72, 74, 89, 90
Orca	26, 29, 30-32
Osprey	16, 21, 49, 57, 59, 67, 69, 70
Peregrine falcon	5, 14, 15, 21, 25, 33, 36
Prairie falcon	52, 75, 76, 80, 81, 87, 90
River otter	4, 20, 30, 37, 42, 59
Rocky Mountain elk	49-51, 53, 57, 73, 89, 90
Roosevelt elk	10, 11, 14, 20, 35, 47
Sandhill crane	1, 3, 7, 79
Sea otter	21, 22
Snow goose	37, 38
Trumpeter swan	11, 12, 19, 37
Tufted puffin	21, 22, 27, 29
Tundra swan	1-3, 7, 37
Western sandpiper	11, 13-15
White pelican	78, 83, 84
White-tailed deer	10, 65-67, 74, 88, 90